The Great Conspiracy - Part III

JOHN ALEXANDER LOGAN

New York 1886

TABLE OF CONTENTS

THE CAUSES OF SECESSION

In preceding Chapters of this work, it has been briefly shown, that from the very hour in which the Republic of the United States was born, there have not been wanting, among its own citizens, those who hated it, and when they could not rule, were always ready to do what they could, by Conspiracy, Sedition, Mutiny, Nullification, Secession, or otherwise, to weaken and destroy it. This fact, and the processes by which the Conspirators worked, is very well stated, in his documentary "History of the Rebellion," by Edward McPherson, when he says: "In the Slaveholding States, a considerable body of men have always been disaffected to the Union. They resisted the adoption of the National Constitution, then sought to refine away the rights and powers of the General Government, and by artful expedients, in a series of years, using the excitements growing out of passing questions, finally perverted the sentiments of large masses of men, and prepared them for Revolution."

Before giving further incontestable proofs establishing this fact, and before endeavoring to sift out the true cause or causes of Secession, let us first examine such evidences as are submitted by him in support of his proposition.

The first piece of testimony, is an extract from an unpublished journal of U. S. Senator Maclay of Pennsylvania, from March 4, 1789, to March 3, 1791—the period of the First Congress under the Federal Constitution. It runs thus:

"1789, June 9.—In relation to the Tariff Bill, the affair of confining the East India Trade to the citizens of America had been negatived, and a committee had been appointed to report on this business. The report came in with

5

very high duties, amounting to a prohibition. But a new phenomenon had made its appearance in the House (meaning the Senate) since Friday.

"Pierce Butler, from South Carolina, had taken his seat, and flamed like a meteor. He arraigned the whole Impost law, and then charged (indirectly) the whole Congress with a design of oppressing South Carolina. He cried out for encouraging the Danes and Swedes, and foreigners of every kind, to come and take away our produce. In fact he was for a Navigation Act reversed.

"June 11.—Attended at the hall as usual.

"Mr. Ralph Izard and Mr. Butler opposed the whole of the drawbacks in every shape whatever.

"Mr. (William) Grayson, of Virginia, warm on this subject, said we were not ripe for such a thing. We were a new Nation, and had no business for any such regulations—a Nation /sui generis/.

"Mr. (Richard Henry) Lee (of Virginia) said drawbacks were right, but would be so much abused, he could not think of admitting them.

"Mr. (Oliver) Ellsworth (of Connecticut) said New England rum would be exported, instead of West India, to obtain the drawback.

"I thought it best to say a few words in reply to each. We were a new Nation, it was true, but we were not a new People. We were composed of individuals of like manners, habits, and customs with the European Nations. What, therefore, had been found useful among them, came well recommended by experience to us. Drawbacks stand as an example in this point of view to us. If the thing was right in itself, there could be no just argument drawn against the use of a thing from the abuse of it. It would be the duty of Government to guard against abuses, by prudent appointments and watchful attention to officers. That as to changing the kind of rum, I thought the collection Bill would provide for this, by limiting the exportation to the original casks and packages. I said a great deal more, but really did not feel much interest either way. But the debates were very lengthy.

"Butler flamed away, and THREATENED A DISSOLUTION OF THE UNION, with regard to his State, as sure as God was in the firmament. He scattered his remarks over the whole Impost bill, calling it partial, oppressive, etc., and solely calculated to oppress South Carolina, and yet ever and anon declaring how clear of local views and how candid and dispassionate he was. He degenerates into mere declamation. His State would live free, or die glorious."

The next piece of evidence is General Jackson's letter to Rev. A. J. Crawford, as follows:

["Private."]

"WASHINGTON, May 1, 1833.

"MY DEAR SIR: * * * I have had a laborious task here, but Nullification is dead; and its actors and courtiers will only be remembered by the People to be execrated for their wicked designs to sever and destroy the only good Government on the globe, and that prosperity and happiness we enjoy over every other portion of the World. Haman's gallows ought to be the fate of all such ambitious men who would involve their Country in Civil War, and all the evils in its train, that they might reign and ride on its whirlwinds and direct the storm. The Free People of these United States have spoken, and consigned these wicked demagogues to their proper doom. Take care of your Nullifiers; you have them among you; let them meet with the indignant frowns of every man who loves his Country. The Tariff, it is now known, was a mere pretext—its burden was on your coarse woolens. By the law of July, 1832, coarse woolen was reduced to five per cent., for the benefit of the South. Mr. Clay's Bill takes it up and classes it with woolens at fifty per cent., reduces it gradually down to twenty per cent., and there it is to remain, and Mr. Calhoun and all the Nullifiers agree to the principle. The cash duties and home valuation will be equal to fifteen per cent. more, and after the year 1842, you pay on coarse woolens thirty-five per cent. If this is not Protection, I cannot understand; therefore the Tariff was only the pretext, and Disunion and a Southern Confederacy the real object. The next pretext will be the Negro or Slavery question.

"My health is not good, but is improving a little. Present me kindly to your lady and family, and believe me to be your friend. I will always be happy to hear from you. "ANDREW JACKSON."

Another evidence is given in the following extract from Benton's "Thirty Years in the Senate," vol. ii., as follows:

"The regular inauguration of this Slavery agitation dates from the year 1835; but it had commenced two years before, and in this way: Nullification and Disunion had commenced in 1830, upon complaint against Protective Tariff. That, being put down in 1833 under President Jackson's proclamation and energetic measures, was immediately substituted by the Slavery agitation. Mr. Calhoun, when he went home from Congress in the spring of that year, told his friends that 'the South could never be united against the North on the Tariff question—that the sugar interest of Louisiana would keep her out—and that the basis of Southern Union must be shifted to the Slave question.' Then all the papers in his interest, and especially the one at Washington, published by Mr. Duff Green, dropped Tariff agitation, and commenced upon Slavery, and in two years had the agitation ripe for inauguration, on the Slavery question. And in tracing this agitation to its present stage, and to comprehend its rationale, it is not to be forgotten that it is a mere continuation of old Tariff Disunion, and preferred because more available."

Again, from p. 490 of his private correspondence, Mr. Clay's words to an Alabamian, in 1844, are thus given:

"From the developments now being made in South Carolina, it is perfectly manifest that a Party exists in that State seeking a Dissolution of the Union, and for that purpose employ the pretext of the rejection of Mr. Tyler's abominable treaty. South Carolina, being surrounded by Slave States, would, in the event of a Dissolution of the Union, suffer only comparative evils; but it is otherwise with Kentucky. She has the boundary of the Ohio extending four hundred miles on three Free States. What would our condition be in the event of the greatest calamity that could befall this Nation?"

Allusion is also made to a letter written by Representative Nathan Appleton, of Boston, December 15, 1860, in which that gentleman said that when he was in Congress—in 1832-33—he had "made up his mind that Messrs. Calhoun, Hayne, McDuffie, etc., were desirous of a separation of the Slave States into a separate Confederacy, as more favorable to the security of Slave Property."

After mentioning that "About 1835, some South Carolinians attempted a Disunion demonstration," our authority says: It is thus described by ex-Governor Francis Thomas of Maryland, in his speech in Baltimore, October 29, 1861:

"Full twenty years ago, when occupying my seat in the House of Representatives, I was surprised one morning, after the assembling of the House, to observe that all the members from the Slaveholding States were absent. Whilst reflecting on this strange occurrence, I was asked why I was not in attendance on the Southern Caucus assembled in the room of the Committee on Claims. I replied that I had received no invitation.

"I then proposed to go to the Committee-room to see what was being done. When I entered, I found that little cock-sparrow, Governor Pickens, of South Carolina, addressing the meeting, and strutting about like a rooster around a barn-yard coop, discussing the following resolution:

"' Resolved, That no member of Congress, representing a Southern constituency, shall again take his seat until a resolution is passed satisfactory to the South on the subject of Slavery.'

"I listened to his language, and when he had finished, I obtained the floor, asking to be permitted to take part in the discussion. I determined at once to kill the Treasonable plot hatched by John C. Calhoun, the Catiline of America, by asking questions. I said to Mr. Pickens, 'What next do you propose we shall do? are we to tell the People that Republicanism is a failure? If you are for that, I am not. I came here to sustain and uphold American institutions; to defend the rights of the North as well as the South; to secure harmony and good fellowship between all Sections of our common Country.' They dared not answer these questions. The Southern temper had not then been gotten up. As my questions were not answered, I moved an adjournment of the Caucus /sine die/. Mr. Craig, of Virginia, seconded the motion, and the company was broken up. We returned to the House, and Mr. Ingersoll, of Pennsylvania, a glorious patriot then as now, introduced a resolution which temporarily calmed the excitement."

The remarks upon this statement, made November 4, 1861, by the National Intelligencer, were as follows:

"However busy Mr. Pickens may have been in the Caucus after it met, the most active man in getting it up and pressing the Southern members to go into it, was Mr. R. B. Rhett, also a member from South Carolina. The occasion, or alleged cause of this withdrawal from the House into secret deliberation was an anti-Slavery speech of Mr. Slade, of Vermont, which Mr. Rhett violently denounced, and proposed to the Southern members to leave the House and go into Conclave in one of the Committee-rooms, which they generally did, if not all of them. We are able to state, however, what may not have been known to Governor Thomas, that at least three besides himself, of those who did attend it, went there with a purpose very different from an intention to consent to any Treasonable measure. These three men were Henry A. Wise, Balie Peyton, and William Cost Johnson. Neither of them opened his lips in the Caucus; they went to observe; and we can assure Governor Thomas, that if Mr. Pickens or Mr. Calhoun, (whom he names) or any one else had presented a distinct proposition looking to Disunion, or Revolt, or Secession, he would have witnessed a scene not soon to be forgotten. The three whom we have mentioned were as brave as they were determined. Fortunately, perhaps, the man whom they went particularly to watch, remained silent and passive."

Let us, however, pursue the inquiry a little further. On the 14th of November, 1860, Alexander H. Stephens addressed the Legislature of Georgia, and in a portion of that address—replying to a speech made before the same Body the previous evening by Mr. Toombs, in which the latter had "recounted the evils of this Government"—said:

"The first [of these evils] was the Fishing Bounties, paid mostly to the sailors of New England. Our friend stated that forty-eight years of our Government was under the administration of Southern Presidents. Well, these Fishing Bounties began under the rule of a Southern President, I believe. No one of them, during the whole forty-eight years, ever set his Administration against the principle or policy of them. * * *

"The next evil which my friend complained of, was the Tariff. Well, let us look at that for a moment. About the time I commenced noticing public matters, this question was agitating the Country almost as fearfully as the Slave question now is. In 1832, when I was in college, South Carolina was ready to Nullify or Secede from the Union on this account. And what have we seen? The Tariff no longer distracts the public counsels. Reason has triumphed! The present Tariff was voted for by Massachusetts and South Carolina. The lion and the lamb lay down together—every man in the

Senate and House from Massachusetts and South Carolina, I think, voted for it, as did my honorable friend himself. And if it be true, to use the figure of speech of my honorable friend, that every man in the North that works in iron, and brass and wood, has his muscle strengthened by the protection of the Government, that stimulant was given by his vote and I believe (that of) every other Southern man.

"Mr. TOOMBS—The Tariff lessened the duties.

"Mr. STEPHENS—Yes, and Massachusetts with unanimity voted with the South to lessen them, and they were made just as low as Southern men asked them to be, and that is the rate they are now at. If reason and argument, with experience, produced such changes in the sentiments of Massachusetts from 1832 to 1857, on the subject of the Tariff, may not like changes be effected there by the same means—reason and argument, and appeals to patriotism on the present vexed question? And who can say that by 1875 or 1890, Massachusetts may not vote with South Carolina and Georgia upon all those questions that now distract the Country and threaten its peace and existence.

"Another matter of grievance alluded to by my honorable friend was the Navigation Laws. This policy was also commenced under the Administration of one of these Southern Presidents who ruled so well, and has been continued through all of them since. * * * One of the objects (of these) was to build up a commercial American marine by giving American bottoms the exclusive Carrying Trade between our own ports. This is a great arm of national power. This object was accomplished. We have now an amount of shipping, not only coastwise, but to foreign countries, which puts us in the front rank of the Nations of the World. England can no longer be styled the Mistress of the Seas. What American is not proud of the result? Whether those laws should be continued is another question. But one thing is certain; no President, Northern or Southern, has ever yet recommended their repeal. * * *

"These then were the true main grievances or grounds of complaint against the general system of our Government and its workings—I mean the administration of the Federal Government. As to the acts of the federal States I shall speak presently: but these three were the main ones used against the common head. Now, suppose it be admitted that all of these are evils in the system; do they overbalance and outweigh the advantages and great good which this same Government affords in a thousand innumerable ways that cannot be estimated? Have we not at the South, as well as the North, grown great, prosperous, and happy under its operations? Has any part of the World ever shown such rapid progress in the development of wealth, and all the material resources of national power and greatness, as the Southern States have under the General Government, notwithstanding all its defects?

"Mr. TOOMBS—In spite of it.

"Mr. STEPHENS—My honorable friend says we have, in spite of the General Government; that without it, I suppose he thinks, we might have done as well, or perhaps better, than we have done in spite of it. * * * Whether we of the South would have been better off without the Government, is, to say the least, problematical. On the one side we can only put the fact, against speculation and conjecture on the other. * * * The influence of the Government on us is like that of the atmosphere around us. Its benefits are so silent and unseen that they are seldom thought of or appreciated.

"We seldom think of the single element of oxygen in the air we breathe, and yet let this simple, unseen and unfelt agent be withdrawn, this life-giving element be taken away from this all-pervading fluid around us, and what instant and appalling changes would take place in all organic creation.

"It may be that we are all that we are 'in spite of the General Government,' but it may be that without it we should have been far different from what we are now. It is true that there is no equal part of the Earth with natural resources superior perhaps to ours. That portion of this Country known as the Southern States, stretching from the Chesapeake to the Rio Grande, is fully equal to the picture drawn by the honorable and eloquent Senator last night, in all natural capacities. But how many ages and centuries passed before these capacities were developed to reach this advanced age of civilization. There these same hills, rich in ore, same rivers, same valleys and plains, are as they have been since they came from the hand of the Creator; uneducated and uncivilized man roamed over them for how long no history informs us.

"It was only under our institutions that they could be developed. Their development is the result of the enterprise of our people, under operations of the Government and institutions under which we have lived. Even our people, without these, never would have done it. The organization of society has much to do with the development of the natural resources of any Country or any Land. The institutions of a People, political and moral, are the matrix in which the germ of their organic structure quickens into life—takes root, and develops in form, nature, and character. Our institutions constitute the basis, the matrix, from which spring all our characteristics of development and greatness. Look at Greece. There is the same fertile soil, the same blue sky, the same inlets and harbors, the same AEgean, the same Olympus; there is the same land where Homer sung, where Pericles spoke; it is in nature the same old Greece—but it is living Greece no more.

"Descendants of the same people inhabit the country; yet what is the reason of this vast difference? In the midst of present degradation we see the glorious fragments of ancient works of art-temples, with ornaments and inscriptions that excite wonder and admiration—the remains of a once high order of civilization, which have outlived the language they spoke—upon them all, Ichabod is written—their glory has departed. Why is this so? I answer, their institutions have been destroyed. These were but the fruits of their forms of government, the matrix from which their great development sprang; and when once the institutions of a People have been destroyed, there is no earthly power that can bring back the Promethean spark to kindle them here again, any more than in that ancient land of eloquence, poetry and song.

"The same may be said of Italy. Where is Rome, once the mistress of the World? There are the same seven hills now, the same soil, the same natural resources; the nature is the same, but what a ruin of human greatness meets the eye of the traveler throughout the length and breadth of that most down-trodden land! why have not the People of that Heaven-favored clime, the spirit that animated their fathers? Why this sad difference?

"It is the destruction of their institutions that has caused it; and, my countrymen, if we shall in an evil hour rashly pull down and destroy those institutions which the patriotic hand of our fathers labored so long and so hard to build up, and which have done so much for us and the World, who can venture the prediction that similar results will not ensue? Let us avoid it if we can. I trust the spirit is among us that will enable us to do it. Let us not rashly try the experiment, for, if it fails, as it did in Greece and Italy, and in the South American Republics, and in every other place wherever liberty is once destroyed, it may never be restored to us again.

"There are defects in our government, errors in administration, and short-comings of many kinds; but in spite of these defects and errors, Georgia has grown to be a great State. Let us pause here a moment.

"When I look around and see our prosperity in everything, agriculture, commerce, art, science, and every department of education, physical and mental, as well as moral advancement—and our colleges—I think, in the face of such an exhibition, if we can, without the loss of power, or any essential right or interest, remain in the Union, it is our duty to ourselves and to posterity—let us not too readily yield to this temptation—to do so. Our first parents, the great progenitors of the human race, were not without a like temptation, when in the Garden of Eden. They were led to believe that their condition would be bettered—that their eyes would be opened— and that they would become as gods. They in an evil hour yielded—instead of becoming gods they only saw their own nakedness.

"I look upon this Country, with our institutions, as the Eden of the World, the Paradise of the Universe. It may be that out of it we may become greater and more prosperous, but I am candid and sincere in telling you that I fear if we rashly evince passion, and without sufficient cause shall take that step, that instead of becoming greater or more peaceful, prosperous, and happy—instead of becoming gods, we will become demons, and at no distant day commence cutting one another's throats. This is my apprehension.

"Let us, therefore, whatever we do, meet those difficulties, great as they are, like wise and sensible men, and consider them in the light of all the consequences which may attend our action. Let us see first clearly where the path of duty leads, and then we may not fear to tread therein."

Said Senator Wigfall, of Texas, March 4, 1861, in the United States Senate, only a few hours before Mr. Lincoln's Inauguration:

"I desire to pour oil on the waters, to produce harmony, peace and quiet here. It is early in the morning, and I hope I shall not say anything that may be construed as offensive. I rise merely that we may have an understanding of this question.

"It is not Slavery in the Territories, it is not expansion, which is the difficulty. If the resolution which the Senator from Wisconsin introduced here, denying the right of Secession, had been adopted by two-thirds of each branch of this department of the Government, and had been ratified by three-fourths of the States, I have no hesitation in saying that, so far as the State in which I live and to which I owe my allegiance is concerned, if she had no other cause for a disruption of the Union taking place, she would undoubtedly have gone out.

[To insert as an additional article of amendment to the Constitution, the following: "Under this Constitution, as originally adopted, and as it now exists, no State has power to withdraw from the jurisdiction of the United States: but this Constitution, and all laws passed in pursuance of its delegated powers, are the Supreme Law of the Land, anything contained in any constitution, ordinance, or act of any State, to the contrary notwithstanding."]

"The moment you deny the right of self-government to the free White men of the South, they will leave the Government. They believe in the Declaration of Independence. They believe that:

"'Governments are instituted among men, deriving their just powers from the consent of the governed; that, whenever any form of government becomes destructive of these ends, it is the right of the People to alter or to abolish it, and to institute a new Government, laying its foundation on such principles and organizing its powers in such form as to them shall seem most likely to effect their safety and happiness.'

"That principle of the Declaration of Independence is the one upon which the free White men of the South predicated their devotion to the present Constitution of the United States; and it was the denial of that, as much as anything else, that has created the dissatisfaction in that Section of the Country.

"There is no instrument of writing that has ever been written that has been

13

more misapprehended and misunderstood and misrepresented than this same unfortunate Declaration of Independence, and no set of gentlemen have ever been so slandered as the fathers who drew and signed that Declaration.

"If there was a thing on earth that they did not intend to assert, it was that a Negro was a White man. As I said here, a short time ago, one of the greatest charges they made against the British Government was, that old King George was attempting to establish the fact practically that all men were created Free and Equal. They charged him in the Declaration of Independence with inciting their Slaves to insurrection. That is one of the grounds upon which they threw off their allegiance to the British Parliament.

"Another great misapprehension is, that the men who drafted that Declaration of Independence had any peculiar fancy for one form of government rather than another. They were not fighting to establish a Democracy in this country; they were not fighting to establish a Republican form of government in this Country. Nothing was further from their intention.

"Alexander Hamilton, after he had fought for seven years, declared that the British form of government was the best that the ingenuity of man had ever devised; and when John Adams said to him, 'without its corruptions;' 'Why,' said he, 'its corruptions are its greatest excellence; without the corruptions, it would be nothing.'

"In the Declaration of Independence, they speak of George III., after this fashion. They say:

"'A prince whose character is thus marked by every act which may define a tyrant, is unfit to be the ruler of a free People.'

"Now, I ask any plain common-sense man what was the meaning of that? Was it that they were opposed to a Monarchical form of government? Was it that they believed a Monarchical form of government was incompatible with civil liberty? No, sir; they entertained no such absurd idea. None of them entertained it; but they say that George III, was a prince whose character was 'marked by every act which may define a tyrant' and that therefore he was 'unfit to be the ruler of a free People.' Had his character not been so marked by every quality which would define a tyrant, he might have been the fit ruler of a free People; ergo, a monarchical form of Government was not incompatible with civil liberty.

"That was clearly the opinion of those men. I do not advocate it now; for I have said frequently that we are wiser than our fathers, and our children will be wiser than we are. One hundred years hence, men will understand their own affairs much better than we do. We understand our affairs better than those who preceded us one hundred years. But what I assert is, that the men of the Revolution did not believe that a Monarchical form of

Government was incompatible with civil liberty.

"What I assert is, that when they spoke of 'all men being created equal,' they were speaking of the White men who then had unsheathed their swords—for what purpose? To establish the right of self-government in themselves; and when they had achieved that, they established, not Democracies, but Republican forms of Government in the thirteen sovereign, separate and independent Colonies. Yet the Declaration of Independence is constantly quoted to prove Negro equality. It proves no such thing; it was intended to prove no such thing.

"The 'glittering generalities' which a distinguished former Senator from Massachusetts (Mr. Choate) spoke of, as contained in the Declaration of Independence, one of them at least, about all men being created equal—was not original with Mr. Jefferson. I recollect seeing a pamphlet called the Principles of the Whigs and Jacobites, published about the year 1745, when the last of the Stuarts, called 'the Pretender,' was striking a blow that was fatal to himself, but a blow for his crown, in which pamphlet the very phraseology is used, word for word and letter for letter. I have not got it here to-night. I sent the other day to the Library to try and find it, but could not find it; it was burnt, I believe, with the pamphlets that were burnt some time ago.

"That Mr. Jefferson copied it or plagiarized it, is not true, I suppose, any more than the charge that the distinguished Senator from New York plagiarized from the Federalist in preparing his celebrated compromising speech which was made here a short time ago. It was the cant phrase of the day in 1745, which was only about thirty years previous to the Declaration of Independence. This particular pamphlet, which I have read, was published; others were published at the same time. That sort of phraseology was used.

"There was a war of classes in England; there were men who were contending for legitimacy; who were contending for the right of the Crown being inherent and depending on the will of God, 'the divine right of Kings,' for maintaining an hereditary landed-aristocracy; there was another Party who were contending against this doctrine of legitimacy, and the right of primogeniture. These were called the Whigs; they established this general phraseology in denouncing the divine right and the doctrine of legitimacy, and it became the common phraseology of the Country; so that in the obscure county of Mecklenburg, in North Carolina, a declaration containing the same assertions was found as in this celebrated Declaration of Independence, written by the immortal Jefferson.

"Which of us, I ask, is there upon this floor who has not read and re-read whatever was written within the last twenty-five or thirty years by the distinguished men of this country? But enough of that.

"As I said before, there ought not have been, and there did not necessarily

15

result from our form of Government, any irrepressible conflict between the Slaveholding and the non-Slaveholding States. Nothing of the sort was necessary.

"Strike out a single clause in the Constitution of the United States, that which secures to each State a Republican form of Government, and there is no reason why, under precisely such a Constitution as we have, States that are Monarchical and States that are Republican, could not live in peace and quiet. They confederate together for common defense and general welfare, each State regulating its domestic concerns in its own way; those which preferred a Republican form of Government maintaining it, and those which preferred a Monarchical form of Government maintaining it.

"But how long could small States, with different forms of Government, live together, confederated for common defense and general welfare, if the people of one Section were to come to the conclusion that their institutions were better than those of the other, and thereupon straightway set about subverting the institutions of the other?"

In the reply of the Rebel "Commissioners of the Southern Confederacy" to Mr. Seward, April 9, 1861, they speak of our Government as being "persistently wedded to those fatal theories of construction of the Federal Constitution always rejected by the statesmen of the South, and adhered to by those of the Administration school, until they have produced their natural and often-predicted result of the destruction of the Union, under which we might have continued to live happily and gloriously together, had the spirit of the ancestry who framed the common Constitution animated the hearts of all their sons."

In the "Address of the people of South Carolina, assembled in Convention, to the people of the Slaveholding States of the United States," by which the attempt was made to justify the passage of the South Carolina Secession Ordinance of 1860, it is declared that:

"Discontent and contention have moved in the bosom of the Confederacy, for the last thirty-five years. During this time South Carolina has twice called her people together in solemn Convention, to take into consideration, the aggressions and unconstitutional wrongs, perpetrated by the people of the North on the people of the South. These wrongs were submitted to by the people of the South, under the hope and expectation that they would be final. But such hope and expectation have proved to be vain. Instead of producing forbearance, our acquiescence has only instigated to new forms of aggressions and outrage; and South Carolina, having again assembled her people in Convention, has this day dissolved her connection with the States constituting the United States.

"The one great evil from which all other evils have flowed, is the overthrow of the Constitution of the United States. The Government of the United States, is no longer the Government of Confederated Republics, but of a consolidated Democracy. It is no longer a free Government, but a Despotism. It is, in fact, such a Government as Great Britain attempted to set over our Fathers; and which was resisted and defeated by a seven years struggle for Independence.

"The Revolution of 1776, turned upon one great principle, self-government,—and self-taxation, the criterion of self-government.

"The Southern States now stand exactly in the same position towards the Northern States, that the Colonies did towards Great Britain. The Northern States, having the majority in Congress, claim the same power of omnipotence in legislation as the British Parliament. 'The General Welfare' is the only limit to the legislation of either; and the majority in Congress, as in the British Parliament, are the sole judges of the expediency of the legislation this 'General Welfare' requires. Thus the Government of the United States has become a consolidated Government; and the people of the Southern States are compelled to meet the very despotism their fathers threw off in the Revolution of 1776.

"The consolidation of the Government of Great Britain over the Colonies, was attempted to be carried out by the taxes. The British Parliament undertook to tax the Colonies to promote British interests. Our fathers resisted this pretension. They claimed the right of self-taxation through their Colonial Legislatures. They were not represented in the British Parliament, and, therefore, could not rightly be taxed by its legislation. The British Government, however, offered them a representation in Parliament; but it was not sufficient to enable them to protect themselves from the majority, and they refused the offer. Between taxation without any representation, and taxation without a representation adequate to protection, there was no difference. In neither case would the Colonies tax themselves. Hence, they refused to pay the taxes laid by the British Parliament.

"And so with the Southern States, towards the Northern States, in the vital matter of taxation. They are in a minority in Congress. Their representation in Congress is useless to protect them against unjust taxation; and they are taxed by the people of the North for their benefit, exactly as the people of Great Britain taxed our ancestors in the British Parliament for their benefit. For the last forty years, the taxes laid by the Congress of the United States have been laid with a view of subserving the interests of the North. The people of the South have been taxed by duties on imports, not for revenue, but for an object inconsistent with revenue—to promote, by prohibitions, Northern interests in the productions of their mines and manufactures.

"There is another evil, in the condition of the Southern towards the Northern States, which our ancestors refused to bear towards Great Britain. Our ancestors not only taxed themselves, but all the taxes collected from them were expended amongst them. Had they submitted to the pretensions of the British Government, the taxes collected from them, would have been expended in other parts of the British Empire. They were fully aware of the effect of such a policy in impoverishing the people from whom taxes are collected, and in enriching those who receive the benefit of their expenditure.

"To prevent the evils of such a policy, was one of the motives which drove them on to Revolution, yet this British policy has been fully realized towards the Southern States, by the Northern States. The people of the Southern States are not only taxed for the benefit of the Northern States, but after the taxes are collected, three fourths of them are expended at the North. This cause, with others, connected with the operation of the General Government, has made the cities of the South provincial. Their growth is paralyzed; they are mere suburbs of Northern cities. The agricultural productions of the South are the basis of the foreign commerce of the United States; yet Southern cities do not carry it on. Our foreign trade is almost annihilated. * * *

"No man can for a moment believe, that our ancestors intended to establish over their posterity, exactly the same sort of Government they had overthrown. * * * Yet by gradual and steady encroachments on the part of the people of the North, and acquiescence on the part of the South, the limitations in the Constitution have been swept away; and the Government of the United States has become consolidated, with a claim of limitless powers in its operations. * * *

"A majority in Congress, according to their interested and perverted views, is omnipotent. * * * Numbers with them, is the great element of free Government. A majority is infallible and omnipotent. 'The right divine to rule in Kings,' is only transferred to their majority. The very object of all Constitutions, in free popular Government, is to restrain the majority. Constitutions, therefore, according to their theory, must be most unrighteous inventions, restricting liberty. None ought to exist; but the body politic ought simply to have a political organization, to bring out and enforce the will of the majority. This theory is a remorseless despotism. In resisting it, as applicable to ourselves, we are vindicating the great cause of free Government, more important, perhaps, to the World, than the existence of all the United States."

In his Special Message to the Confederate Congress at Montgomery, April 29, 1861, Mr. Jefferson Davis said:

"From a period as early as 1798, there had existed in all the States a Party, almost uninterruptedly in the majority, based upon the creed that each State was, in the last resort, the sole judge, as well of its wrongs as of the mode and measure of redress. * * * The Democratic Party of the United States repeated, in its successful canvas of 1836, the declaration, made in numerous previous political contests, that it would faithfully abide by and

18

uphold the principles laid down in the Kentucky and Virginia Legislatures of [1798 and] 1799, and that it adopts those principles as constituting one of the main foundations of its political creed."

In a letter addressed by the Rebel Commissioners in London (Yancey, Rost and Mann), August 14, 1861, to Lord John Russell, Secretary of Foreign Affairs, it appears that they said: "It was from no fear that the Slaves would be liberated, that Secession took place. The very Party in power has proposed to guarantee Slavery forever in the States, if the South would but remain in the Union." On the 4th of May preceding, Lord John had received these Commissioners at his house; and in a letter of May 11, 1861, wrote, from the Foreign Office, to Lord Lyons, the British Minister at Washington, a letter, in which, alluding to his informal communication with them, he said: "One of these gentlemen, speaking for the others, dilated on the causes which had induced the Southern States to Secede from the Northern. The principal of these causes, he said, was not Slavery, but the very high price which, for the sake of Protecting the Northern manufacturers, the South were obliged to pay for the manufactured goods which they required. One of the first acts of the Southern Congress was to reduce these duties, and to prove their sincerity he gave as an instance that Louisiana had given up altogether that Protection on her sugar which she enjoyed by the legislation of the United States. As a proof of the riches of the South. He stated that of $350,000,000 of exports of produce to foreign countries $270,000,000 were furnished by the Southern States." * * * They pointed to the new Tariff of the United States as a proof that British manufactures would be nearly excluded from the North, and freely admitted in the South.

This may be as good a place as any other to say a few words touching another alleged "cause" of Secession. During the exciting period just prior to the breaking out of the great War of the Rebellion, the Slave-holding and Secession-nursing States of the South, made a terrible hubbub over the Personal Liberty Bills of the Northern States. And when Secession came, many people of the North supposed these Bills to be the prime, if not the only real cause of it. Not so. They constituted, as we now know, only a part of the mere pretext. But, none the less, they constituted a portion of the history of that eventful time, and cannot be altogether ignored.

In order then, that the reader may quickly grasp, not only the general nature, but also the most important details of the Personal Liberty Bills (in force, in 1860, in many of the Free States) so frequently alluded to in the Debates of Congress, in speeches on the stump, and in the fulminations of Seceding States and their authorized agents, commissioners, and representatives, it may be well now, briefly to refer to them, and to state that no such laws existed in California, Illinois, Indiana, Iowa, Minnesota, New York, Ohio and Oregon.

Those of Maine provided that no officer of the State should in any way assist in the arrest or detention of a Fugitive Slave, and made it the duty of county attorneys to defend the Fugitive Slave against the claim of his master. A Bill to repeal these laws passed the Maine Senate, but failed in the House.

That of Massachusetts provided for commissioners in each county to defend alleged Fugitives from Service or Labor; for payment by the Commonwealth of all expenses of defense; prohibited the issue or service of process by State officers for arrest of alleged Fugitives, or the use of any prisons in the State for their detention, or that of any person aiding their escape; prohibited the kidnapping or removal of alleged Fugitive Slaves by any person; prohibited all officers within the State, down to Town officers, from arresting, imprisoning, detaining or returning to Service "any Person for the reason that he is claimed or adjudged to be a Fugitive from Service or Labor"—all such prohibitions being enforced by heavy fines and imprisonment. The Act of March 25, 1861, materially modified and softened the above provisions.

New Hampshire's law, provided that all Slaves entering the State with consent of the master shall be Free, and made the attempt to hold any person as a Slave within the State a felony.

Vermont's, prescribed that no process under the Fugitive Slave Law should be recognized by any of her Courts, officers, or citizens; nor any aid given in arresting or removing from the State any Person claimed as a Fugitive Slave; provided counsel for alleged Fugitives; for the issue of habeas corpus and trial by jury of issues of fact between the parties; ordained Freedom to all within the State who may have been held as Slaves before coming into it, and prescribed heavy penalties for any attempt to return any such to Slavery. A bill to repeal these laws, proposed November, 1860, in the Vermont House of Representatives, was beaten by two to one.

Connecticut's, provided that there must be two witnesses to prove that a Person is a Slave; that depositions are not evidence; that false testifying in Fugitive Slave cases shall be punishable by fine of $5,000 and five years in State prison.

In New Jersey, the only laws touching the subject, permitted persons temporarily sojourning in the State to bring and hold their Slaves, and made it the duty of all State officers to aid in the recovery of Fugitives from Service.

In Pennsylvania, barring an old dead-letter Statute, they simply prohibited any interference by any of the Courts, Aldermen, or Justices of the Peace, of the Commonwealth, with the functions of the Commissioner appointed under the United States Statute in Fugitive Slave cases.

In Michigan, the law required States' attorneys to defend Fugitive Slaves; prescribed the privileges of habeas corpus and jury trial for all such arrested;

prohibited the use of prisons of the State for their detention; required evidence of two credible witnesses as to identity; and provided heavy penalties of fine and imprisonment for the seizure of any Free Person, with intent to have such Person held in Slavery. A Bill to repeal the Michigan law was defeated in the House by about two to one.

Wisconsin's Personal Liberty law was similar to that of Michigan, but with this addition, that no judgment recovered against any person in that State for violating the Fugitive Slave Law of 1850 should be enforced by sale or execution of any real or personal property in that State.

That of Rhode Island, forbade the carrying away of any Person by force out of the State; forbade the official aiding in the arrest or detention of a Fugitive Slave; and denied her jails to the United States for any such detention.

Apropos of this subject, and before leaving it, it may be well to quote remarks of Mr. Simons of Rhode Island, in the United States Senate. Said he: "Complaint has been made of Personal Liberty Bills. Now, the Massachusetts Personal Liberty Bill was passed by a Democratic House, a Democratic Senate, and signed by a Democratic Governor, a man who was afterwards nominated by Mr. Polk for the very best office in New England, and was unanimously confirmed by a Democratic United States Senate. Further than this, the very first time the attention of the Massachusetts Legislature was called to the propriety of a repeal of this law was by a Republican Governor. Now, on the other hand, South Carolina had repealed a law imprisoning British colored sailors, but retained the one imprisoning those coming from States inhabited by her own brethren!"

These Personal Liberty Bills were undoubtedly largely responsible for some of the irritation on the Slavery question preceding open hostilities between the Sections. But President Lincoln sounded the real depths of the Rebellion when he declared it to be a War upon the rights of the People. In his First Annual Message, December 3, 1861, he said:

"It continues to develop that the insurrection is largely, if not exclusively, a War upon the first principle of popular government—the rights of the People. Conclusive evidence of this is found in the most grave and maturely considered public documents, as well as in the general tone of the insurgents. In those documents we find the abridgment of the existing right of suffrage, and the denial to the People of all right to participate in the selection of public officers, except the legislative, boldly advocated, with labored arguments to prove that large control of the People in government is the source of all political evil. Monarchy itself is sometimes hinted at as a possible refuge from the power of the People.

"In my present position, I could scarcely be justified were I to omit raising a warning voice against this approach of returning despotism.

"It is not needed, nor fitting here, that a general argument should be made in favor of popular institutions; but there is one point, with its connections, not so hackneyed as most others, to which I ask brief attention. It is the effort to place Capital on an equal footing with, if not above Labor, in the structure of the Government.

"It is assumed that Labor is available only in connection with Capital; that nobody labors unless somebody else, owning Capital, somehow by the use of it induces him to labor. This assumed, it is next considered whether it is best that Capital shall hire laborers, and thus induce them to work by their own consent, or buy them, and drive them to it without their consent. Having proceeded so far, it is naturally concluded that all laborers are either hired laborers, or what we call Slaves. And further, it is assumed that whoever is once a hired laborer is fixed in that condition for life.

"Now, there is no such relation between Capital and Labor as assumed; nor is there any such thing as a free man being fixed for life, in the condition of a hired laborer. Both these assumptions are false, and all inferences from them are groundless.

"Labor is prior to, and independent of Capital. Capital is only the fruit of Labor, and could never have existed if Labor had not first existed. Labor is the superior of Capital, and deserves much the higher consideration. Capital has its rights, which are as worthy of protection as any other rights. Nor is it denied that there is, and probably always will be, a relation between Labor and Capital, producing mutual benefits. The error is in assuming that the whole Labor of the community exists within that relation.

"A few men own Capital, and that few, avoid labor themselves, and with their Capital hire or buy another few to labor for them. A large majority belong to neither class—neither work for others, nor have others working for them.

"In most of the Southern States, a majority of the whole people of all colors are neither Slaves nor masters; while in the Northern, a large majority are neither hirers nor hired. Men with their families—wives, sons, and daughters—work for themselves, on their farms, in their houses, and in their shops, taking the whole product to themselves, and asking no favors of Capital on the one hand, nor of hired laborers or Slaves on the other.

"It is not forgotten that a considerable number of persons mingle their own Labor with Capital—that is they labor with their own hands, and also buy or hire others to labor for them; but this is only a mixed, and not a distinct class. No principle stated is disturbed by the existence of this mixed class.

"Again, as has already been said, there is not, of necessity, any such thing as the free hired-laborer being fixed to that condition for life. Many independent men everywhere in these States, a few years back in their lives, were hired laborers.

"The prudent, penniless beginner in the World, labors for wages awhile, saves a surplus with which to buy tools or land for himself, then labors on his own account another while, and at length hires another new beginner to help him. This is the just and generous and prosperous system, which opens the way to all, gives hope to all, and consequent energy and progress, and improvement of condition to all.

"No men living are more worthy to be trusted than those who toil up from poverty—none less inclined to take or touch aught which they have not honestly earned. Let them beware of surrendering a political power which they already possess, and which, if surrendered, will surely be used to close the door of advancement against such as they, and to fix new disabilities and burdens upon them, till all of Liberty shall be lost. * * * The struggle of to-day is not altogether for to-day-it is a vast future also. * * * "

So too, Andrew Johnson, in his speech before the Senate, January 31, 1862, spake well and truly when he said that "there has been a deliberate design for years to change the nature and character and genius of this Government." And he added: "Do we not know that these schemers have been deliberately at work, and that there is a Party in the South, with some associates in the North, and even in the West, that have become tired of Free Government, in which they have lost confidence."

Said he: "They raise an outcry against 'Coercion,' that they may paralyze the Government, cripple the exercise of the great powers with which it was invested, finally to change its form and subject us to a Southern despotism. Do we not know it to be so? Why disguise this great truth? Do we not know that they have been anxious for a change of Government for years? Since this Rebellion commenced it has manifested itself in many quarters.

"How long is it since the organ of the Government at Richmond, the Richmond Whig, declared that rather than live under the Government of the United States, they preferred to take the Constitutional Queen of Great Britain as their protector; that they would make an alliance with Great Britain for the purpose of preventing the enforcement of the Laws of the United States. Do we not know this?"

Stephen A. Douglas also, in his great Union speech at Chicago, May 1, 1861—only a few days before his lamented death—said:

"The election of Mr. Lincoln is a mere pretext. The present Secession movement is the result of an enormous Conspiracy formed more than a year since formed by leaders in the Southern Confederacy more than twelve months ago. They use the Slavery question as a means to aid the accomplishment of their ends. They desired the election of a Northern candidate by a Sectional vote, in order to show that the two Sections cannot live together.

"When the history of the two years from the Lecompton question down to the Presidential election shall be written, it will be shown that the scheme was deliberately made to break up this Union.

"They desired a Northern Republican to be elected by a purely Northern vote, and then assign this fact as a reason why the Sections cannot live together. If the Disunion candidate—(Breckinridge) in the late Presidential contest had carried the united South, their scheme was, the Northern candidate successful, to seize the Capital last Spring, and by a united South and divided North, hold it.

"Their scheme was defeated, in the defeat of the Disunion candidates in several of the Southern States.

"But this is no time for a detail of causes. The Conspiracy is now known; Armies have been raised. War is levied to accomplish it. There are only two sides to the question.

"Every man must be for the United States, or against it. There can be no Neutrals in this War; only Patriots or Traitors! [Cheer after Cheer]."

In a speech made in the United States Senate, January 31, 1862, Senator McDougall of California—conceded to be intellectually the peer of any man in that Body—said:

"We are at War. How long have we been at War? We have been engaged in a war of opinion, according to my historical recollection, since 1838. There has been a Systematic organized war against the Institutions established by our fathers, since 1832. This is known of all men who have read carefully the history of our Country. If I had the leisure, or had consulted the authorities, I would give it year by year, and date by date, from that time until the present, how men adversary to our Republican Institutions have been organizing War against us, because they did not approve of our Republican Institutions.

"Before the Mexican War, it is well known that General Quitman, then Governor of Mississippi, was organizing to produce the same condition of things (and he hoped a better condition of things, for he hoped a successful Secession), to produce this same revolution that is now disturbing our whole Land. The War with Mexico, fighting for a Southern proposition, for which I fought myself, made the Nation a unit until 1849; and then again they undertook an Organization to produce Revolution. These things are history. This statement is true, and cannot be denied among intelligent men anywhere, and cannot be denied in this Senate.

"The great men who sat in Council in this Hall, the great men of the Nation, men whose equals are not, and I fear will not be for many years, uniting their judgments, settled the controversy in 1850. They did not settle it for the Conspirators of the South, for they were not parties to the compact. Clay and Webster, and the great men who united with them, had no relation with the extremes of either extreme faction. The Compromise was made, and immediately after it had been effected, again commenced the work of organization. I had the honor to come from my State on the Pacific into the other branch of the Federal Congress, and there I learned as early as 1853, that the work of Treason was as industriously pursued as it is being pursued to-day. I saw it; I felt it; I knew it. I went home to the shores of the Pacific instructed somewhat on this subject.

"Years passed by. I engaged in my duties as a simple professional man, not connected with public affairs. The question of the last Presidential election arose before the Country—one of those great questions that are not appreciated, I regret from my heart, by the American Nation, when we elect a President, a man who has more power for his time than any enthroned Monarch in Europe. We organize a Government and place him in front as the head and the Chief of the Government. That question came before the American People.

"At that time I was advised of this state of feeling—and I will state it in as exact form of words as I can state it, that it may be understood by Senators: Mr. Douglas is a man acceptable to the South. Mr. Douglas is a man to whom no one has just cause of exception throughout the South. Mr. Douglas is more acceptable to Mississippi and Louisiana than Mr. Breckinridge. Mr. Breckinridge is not acceptable to the South; or at least, if he is so, he is not in the same degree with Mr. Douglas. Mr. Douglas is the accepted man of a great National Party, and if he is brought into the field he will be triumphantly elected. THAT MUST NOT BE DONE, because THE ORGANIZATION FOR SECESSION IS MATURED. EVERYTHING IS PREPARED, and the election of Mr. Douglas would only postpone it for four years; and Now when we are PREPARED to carry out these things WE MUST INDULGE IN STRATAGEM, and the nomination of Mr. Breckinridge is a mere strategic movement to divide the great conservative Party of the Nation into two, so as to elect a Republican candidate AND CONSOLIDATE THE SOUTH BY THE CRY OF 'ABOLITIONIST!'

"That is a mere simple statement of the truth, and it cannot be contradicted. Now, in that scheme all the men of counsel of that Party were engaged. * * * I, on the far shores of the Pacific understood those things as long ago as a year last September (1860). I was advised about this policy and well informed of it. * * *

"I was at war, in California, in January (1861) last; in the maintenance of the opinions that I am now maintaining, I had to go armed to protect myself from violence. The country, whenever there was controversy, was agitated to its deepest foundations. That is known, perhaps, not to gentlemen who live up in Maine or Massachusetts, or where you are foreign to all this agitation; but known to all people where disturbance might have been effective in consequences. I felt it, and had to carry my life in my hand by the month, as did my friends surrounding me.

"I say that all through last winter (that of 1860-61) War had been inaugurated in all those parts of the Country where disturbed elements could have efficient result. In January (1861), a year ago, I stood in the hall of the House of Representatives of my State, and there was War then, and angry faces and hostile men were gathered; and we knew then well that the Southern States had determined to withdraw themselves from the Federal Union.

"I happened to be one of those men who said, 'they shall not do it;' and it appears to me that the whole argument is between that class of men and the class of men who said they would let them do it. * * * When this doctrine was started here of disintegrating the Cotton States from the rest of the Confederacy, I opposed it at once. I saw immediately that War was to be invoked. * * *

"I will not say these things were understood by gentlemen of the Republican Party * * * but I, having been accepted and received as a Democrat of the old school from the olden time, and HAVING FAST SOUTHERN SYMPATHIES, I DID KNOW ALL ABOUT THEM. * * * I KNOW THAT SECESSION WAS A THING DETERMINED UPON. * * * I was advised of and understood the whole programme, KNEW HOW IT WAS TO BE DONE IN ITS DETAILS; and I being advised, made war against it. * * *

"War had been, in fact, inaugurated. What is War? Was it the firing on our flag at Sumter? Was that the first adversary passage? To say so, is trifling with men's judgments and information. No, sir; when they organized a Government, and set us at defiance, they commenced War; and the various steps they took afterwards, by organizing their troops, and forming their armies, and advancing upon Sumter; all these were merely acts of War; but War was inaugurated whenever they undertook to say they would maintain themselves as a separate and independent government; and, after that time, every man who gave his assistance to them was a Traitor, according to the highest Law."

The following letter, written by one of the most active of the Southern conspirators in 1858, during the great Douglas and Lincoln Debate of that year, to which extended reference has already been made, is of interest in this connection, not only as corroborative evidence of the fact that the Rebellion of the Cotton States had been determined on long before Mr. Lincoln was elected President, but as showing also that the machinery for "firing the Southern heart" and for making a "solid South" was being perfected even then. The subsequent split in the Democratic Party, and nomination of Breckinridge by the Southern wing of it, was managed by this same Yancey, simply as parts of the deliberate programme of Secession and Rebellion long before determined on by the Cotton Lords of the Cotton States.

"MONTGOMERY, June 15, 1858.

"DEAR SIR:—Your kind favor of the 13th is received.

"I hardly agree with you that a general movement can be made that will clean out the Augean Stable. If the Democracy were overthrown it would result in giving place to a greedier and hungrier swarm of flies.

"The remedy of the South is not in such a process. It is in a diligent organization of her true men for prompt resistance to the next aggression. It must come in the nature of things. No National Party can save us. No Sectional Party can ever do it. But if we could do as our fathers did— organize 'Committees of Safety' all over the Cotton States (and it is only in them that we can hope for any effective movement), we shall fire the Southern heart, instruct the Southern mind, give courage to each other, and at the proper moment, by one organized, concerted action, we can precipitate the Cotton States into a revolution.

"The idea has been shadowed forth in the South by Mr. Ruffin; has been taken up and recommended in the Advertiser under the name of 'League of United Southerners,' who, keeping up their old relations on all other questions, will hold the Southern issues paramount, and influence parties, legislatures and statesmen. I have no time to enlarge, but to suggest merely.

"In haste, yours, etc. "W. L. YANCEY.

"To JAMES S. SLAUGHTER."

At Jackson, Mississippi, in the fall of the same year (1858) just after the great Debate between Douglas and Lincoln had closed, Jefferson Davis had already raised the standard of Revolution, Secession and Disunion, during the course of a speech, in which he said: "If an Abolitionist be chosen President of the United States, you will have presented to you the question of whether you will permit the Government to pass into the hands of your avowed and implacable enemies? Without pausing for an answer, I will state my own position to be, that such a result would be a species of revolution by which the purposes of the Government would be destroyed, and the observance of its mere forms entitled to no respect. In that event, in such a manner as should be most expedient, I should deem it your duty to provide for your safety, outside of the Union with those who have already shown the will, and would have acquired the power to deprive you of your birthright, and to reduce you to worse than the Colonial dependence of your fathers."

The "birthright" thus referred to was of course, the alleged right to have Slaves; but what was this "worse than Colonial dependence" to which, in addition to the peril supposed to threaten the Southern "birthright," the Cotton States of Mississippi were reduced? "Dependence" upon whom, and with regard to what? Plainly upon the North; and with regard, not to Slavery alone—for Jefferson Davis held, down to the very close of the War, that the South fought "not for Slavery"—but as to Tariff Legislation also. There was the rub! These Cotton Lords believed, or pretended to believe, that the High Tariff Legislation, advocated and insisted upon both by the Whigs and Republicans for the Protection of the American Manufacturer and working man, built up and made prosperous the North, and elevated Northern laborers; at the expense of the South, and especially themselves, the Cotton Lords aforesaid.

We have already seen from the utterances of leading men in the South Carolina, Secession Convention, "that"—as Governor Hicks, himself a Southern man, said in his address to the people of Maryland, after the War broke out "neither the election of Mr. Lincoln, nor the non-execution of the Fugitive Slave Law, nor both combined, constitute their grievances. They declare that THE REAL CAUSE of their discontent DATES AS FAR BACK AS 1833."

And what was the chief cause or pretext for discontent at that time? Nothing less than the Tariff. They wanted Free Trade, as well as Slavery. The balance of the Union wanted Protection, as well as Freedom.

The subsequent War, then, was not a War waged for Slavery alone, but for Independence with a view to Free Trade, as set forth in the "Confederate Constitution," as soon as that Independence could be achieved. And the War on our part, while for the integrity of the Union in all its parts—for the life of the Nation itself, and for the freedom of man, should also have brought the triumph of the American idea of a Protective Tariff, whose chief object is the building up of American manufactures and the Protection of the Free working-man, in the essential matters of education, food, clothing, rents, wages, and work.

It is mentioned in McPherson's History of the Rebellion, p. 392, that in a letter making public his reasons for going to Washington and taking his seat in Congress, Mr. James L. Pugh, a Representative from Alabama, November 24, 1860, said: "The sole object of my visit is to promote the cause of Secession."

From the manner in which they acted after reaching Washington, it is not unreasonable to suppose that most of those persons representing, in both branches of Congress, the Southern States which afterwards seceded, came to the National Capital with a similar object in view—taking their salaries and mileages for services supposed to be performed for the benefit of the very Government they were conspiring to injure, and swearing anew the sacred oath to support and defend the very Constitution which they were moving heaven and earth to undermine and destroy!

[As a part of the history of those times, the following letter is not without interest:

"OXFORD, December 24, 1860.

"MY DEAR SIR:—I regretted having to leave Washington without having with you a full conference as to the great events whose shadows are upon us. The result of the election here is what the most sanguine among us expected; that is, its general result is so. It is as yet somewhat difficult to determine the distinctive complexion of the convention to meet on the 7th of January. The friends of Southern Independence, of firm and bona fide resistance, won an overwhelming victory; but I doubt whether there is any precise plan.

"No doubt a large majority of the Convention will be for separate Secession. But unless intervening events work important changes of sentiment, not all of those elected as resistance men will be for immediate and separate Secession. Our friends in Pontotoc, Tippah, De Soto and Pauola took grounds which fell far short of that idea, though their resolutions were very firm in regard to Disunion and an ultimate result.

"In the meantime the Disunion sentiment among the people is growing every day more intense.

"Upon the whole, you have great cause for gratification in the action of your State.

"The submissionists are routed, horse, foot, and dragoons, and any concession by the North will fail to restore that sacred attachment to the Union which was once so deeply radicated in the hearts of our people. What they want now, is wise and sober leading. I think that there might be more of dignity and prudent foresight in the action of our State than have marked the proceedings of South Carolina. I have often rejoiced that we have you to rest upon and confide in. I do not know what we could do without you. That God may preserve you to us, and that your mind may retain all its vigor to carry us through these perilous times, is my most fervent aspiration.

"I am as ever, and forever, your supporter, ally and friend.

"L. Q. C. LAMAR.

"COL. JEFF. DAVIS, Washington, D. C."]

This was but a part of the deliberate, cold-blooded plan mapped out in detail, early in the session succeeding the election of Mr. Lincoln, in a secret Caucus of the Chief Plotters of the Treason. It was a secret conference, but the programme resolved on, soon leaked out.

The following, which appeared in the Washington National Intelligencer on Friday, January 11, 1861, tells the story of this stage of the Great Conspiracy pretty clearly:

"The subjoined communication, disclosing the designs of those who have undertaken to lead the movement now threatening a permanent dissolution of the Union, comes to us from a distinguished citizen of the South [understood to be Honorable Lemuel D. Evans, Representative from Texas in the 34th Congress, from March 4, 1855, to March 3, 1857] who formerly represented his State with great distinction in the popular branch of Congress.

"Temporarily sojourning in this city he has become authentically informed of the facts recited in the subjoined letter, which he communicates to us under a sense of duty, and for the accuracy of which he makes himself responsible.

"Nothing but assurances coming from such an intelligent, reliable source could induce us to accept the authenticity of these startling statements, which so deeply concern not only the welfare but the honor of the Southern people.

"To them we submit, without present comment, the programme to which they are expected to yield their implicit adhesion, without any scruples of conscience as without any regard for their own safety.

"'WASHINGTON, January 9, 1861.

"'I charge that on last Saturday night (January 5th), a Caucus was held in this city by the Southern Secession Senators from Florida, Georgia, Alabama, Mississippi, Louisiana, Arkansas and Texas. It was then and there resolved in effect to assume to themselves the political power of the South, and, to control all political and military operations for the present, they telegraphed to complete the plan of seizing forts, arsenals, and custom-houses, and advised the Conventions now in session, and soon to assemble, to pass Ordinances for immediate Secession; but, in order to thwart any operations of the Government here, the Conventions of the Seceding States are to retain their representations in the Senate and the House.

"'They also advised, ordered, or directed the assembling of a Convention of delegates from the Seceding States at Montgomery on the 13th of February. This can of course only be done by the revolutionary Conventions usurping the powers of the people, and sending delegates over whom they will lose all control in the establishment of a Provisional Government, which is the plan of the dictators.

"'This Caucus also resolved to take the most effectual means to dragoon the Legislatures of Tennessee, Kentucky, Missouri, Arkansas, Texas, and Virginia into following the Seceding States. Maryland is also to be influenced by such appeals to popular passion as have led to the revolutionary steps which promise a conflict with the State and Federal Governments in Texas.

"'They have possessed themselves of all the avenues of information in the South—the telegraph, the press, and the general control of the postmasters. They also confidently rely upon defections in the army and navy.

"'The spectacle here presented is startling to contemplate. Senators entrusted with the representative sovereignty of the States, and sworn to support the Constitution of the United States, while yet acting as the privy councillors of the President, and anxiously looked to by their constituents to effect some practical plan of adjustment, deliberately conceive a Conspiracy for the overthrow of the Government through the military organizations, the dangerous secret order, the 'Knights of the Golden Circle,' 'Committees of Safety,' Southern leagues, and other agencies at their command; they have instituted as thorough a military and civil despotism as ever cursed a maddened Country.

"'It is not difficult to foresee the form of government which a Convention thus hurriedly thrown together at Montgomery will irrevocably fasten upon a deluded and unsuspecting people. It must essentially be 'a Monarchy founded upon military principles,' or it cannot endure. Those who usurp power never fail to forge strong chains.

"'It may be too late to sound the alarm. Nothing may be able to arrest the action of revolutionary tribunals whose decrees are principally in 'secret sessions.' But I call upon the people to pause and reflect before they are forced to surrender every principle of liberty, or to fight those who are becoming their masters rather than their servants. '" EATON"

"As confirming the intelligence furnished by our informant we may cite the following extract from the Washington correspondence of yesterday's Baltimore Sun:

"'The leaders of the Southern movement are consulting as to the best mode of consolidating their interests into a Confederacy under a Provisional Government. The plan is to make Senator Hunter, of Virginia, Provisional President, and Jefferson Davis Commander-in-Chief of the army of defense. Mr. Hunter possesses in a more eminent degree the philosophical characteristics of Jefferson than any other statesman now living. Colonel Davis is a graduate of West Point, was distinguished for gallantry at Buena Vista, and served as Secretary of War under President Pierce, and is not second to General Scott in military science or courage.'

"As further confirmatory of the above, the following telegraphic dispatch in the Charleston Mercury of January 7, 1861, is given:

"'[From our Own Correspondent.]

"'WASHINGTON, January 6.—The Senators from those of the Southern States which have called Conventions of their people, met in caucus last night, and adopted the following resolutions:

"'Resolved, That we recommend to our respective States immediate Secession.

"'Resolved, That we recommend the holding of a General Convention of the said States, to be holden in the city of Montgomery, Alabama, at some period not later than the 15th day of February, 1861.'

"These resolutions were telegraphed this evening to the Conventions of Alabama, Mississippi, and Florida. A third resolution is also known to have been adopted, but it is of a confidential character, not to be divulged at present. There was a good deal of discussion in the caucus on the question of whether the Seceding States ought to continue their delegations in Congress till the 4th of March, to prevent unfriendly legislation, or whether the Representatives of the Seceding States should all resign together, and leave a clear field for the opposition to pass such bills, looking to Coercion, as they may see fit. It is believed that the opinion that they should remain prevailed."

Furthermore, upon the capture of Fernandina, Florida, in 1862, the following letter was found and published. Senator Yulee, the writer, was present and participated as one of the Florida Senators, in the traitorous "Consultation" therein referred to—and hence its especial value:

"WASHINGTON, January 7, 1861.

"My DEAR SIR:—On the other side is a copy of resolutions adopted at a consultation of the Senators from the Seceding States—in which Georgia, Alabama, Louisiana, Arkansas, Texas, Mississippi, and Florida were present.

"The idea of the meeting was that the States should go out at once, and provide for the early organization of a Confederate Government, not later than 15th February. This time is allowed to enable Louisiana and Texas to participate. It seemed to be the opinion that if we left here, force, loan, and volunteer Bills might be passed, which would put Mr. Lincoln in immediate condition for hostilities; whereas, by remaining in our places until the 4th of March, it is thought we can keep the hands of Mr. Buchanan tied, and disable the Republicans from effecting any legislation which will strengthen the hands of the incoming Administration.

"The resolutions will be sent by the delegation to the President of the Convention. I have not been able to find Mr. Mallory (his Senatorial colleague) this morning. Hawkins (Representative from Florida) is in Connecticut. I have therefore thought it best to send you this copy of the resolutions.

"In haste, yours truly "D. L. YULEE.

"JOSEPH FINEGAN, Esq., "'Sovereignty Convention,' Tallahassee, Fla."

The resolutions "on the other side" of this letter, to which he refers, are as follows:

"Resolved, 1—That in our opinion each of the Southern States should, as soon as may be, Secede from the Union.

"Resolved, 2—That provision should be made for a Convention to organize a Confederacy of the Seceding States, the Convention to meet not later than the 15th of February, at the city of Montgomery, in the State of Alabama.

"Resolved, That in view of the hostile legislation that is threatened against the Seceding States, and which may be consummated before the 4th of March, we ask instructions whether the delegations are to remain in Congress until that date for the purpose of defeating such legislation.

"Resolved, That a committee be and are hereby appointed, consisting of Messrs. Davis, Slidell, and Mallory, to carry out the objects of this meeting."

In giving this letter to the World—from its correspondent accompanying the expedition—the New York Times of March 15, 1862, made these forcible and clear-headed comments:

"The telegraphic columns of the Times of January 7, 1861, contained the following Washington dispatch: 'The Southern Senators last night (January 5th) held a conference, and telegraphed to the Conventions of their respective States to advise immediate Secession.' Now, the present letter is a report by Mr. Yulee, who was present at this 'consultation' as he calls it, of the resolutions adopted on this occasion, transmitted to the said Finegan, who by the way, was a member of the 'Sovereign Convention' of Florida, then sitting in the town of Tallahassee.

"It will thus be seen that this remarkable letter, which breathes throughout the spirit of the Conspirator, in reality lets us into one of the most important of the numerous Secret Conclaves which the Plotters of Treason then held in the Capital. It was then, as it appears, that they determined to strike the blow and precipitate their States into Secession. But at the same time they resolved that it would be imprudent for them openly to withdraw, as in that case Congress might pass 'force, loan, and volunteer bills,' which would put Mr. Lincoln in immediate condition for hostilities. No, no! that would not do. (So much patriotic virtue they half suspected, half feared, was left in the Country.) On the contrary, 'by remaining in our places until the 4th of March it is thought we can keep the hands of Mr. Buchanan tied, and disable the Republicans from effecting any legislation which will strengthen the hands of the incoming Administration.' Ah what a tragic back-ground, full of things unutterable, is there!

"It appears, however, that events were faster than they, and instead of being able to retain their seats up to the 4th of March, they were able to remain but a very few weeks. Mr. Davis withdrew on the 21st of January, just a fortnight after this 'consultation.' But for the rest, mark how faithfully the programme here drawn up by this knot of Traitors in secret session was realized. Each of the named States represented by this Cabal did, 'as soon as may be, Secede from the Union'—the Mississippi Convention passing its Ordinance on the heels of the receipt of these resolutions, on the 9th of January; Florida and Alabama on the 11th; Louisiana on the 26th, and Texas on the 1st of February; while the 'organization of the Confederate Government' took place at the very time appointed, Davis being inaugurated on the 18th of February.

"And here is another Plot of the Traitors brought to light. These very men, on withdrawing from the Senate, urged that they were doing so in obedience to the command of their respective States. As Mr. Davis put it, in his parting speech, 'the Ordinance of Secession having passed the Convention of his State, he felt obliged to obey the summons, and retire from all official connection with the Federal Government.' This letter of Mr. Yulee's clearly reveals that they had themselves pushed their State Conventions to the adoption of the very measure which they had the hardihood to put forward as an imperious 'summons' which they could not disobey. It is thus that Treason did its Work."

COPPERHEADISM VS. UNION DEMOCRACY

When we remember that it was on the night of the 5th of January, 1861, that the Rebel Conspirators in the United States Senate met and plotted their confederated Treason, as shown in the Yulee letter, given in the preceding Chapter of this work, and that on the very next day, January 6, 1861, Fernando Wood, then Mayor of the great city of New York, sent in to the Common Council of that metropolis, his recommendation that New York city should Secede from its own State, as well as the United States, and become "a Free City," which, said he, "may shed the only light and hope of a future reconstruction of our once blessed Confederacy," it is impossible to resist the conviction that this extraordinary movement of his, was inspired and prompted, if not absolutely directed, by the secret Rebel Conclave at Washington. It bears within itself internal evidences of such prompting.

Thus, when Mayor Wood states the case in the following words, he seems to be almost quoting word for word an instruction received by him from these Rebel leaders—in connection with their plausible argument, upholding it. Says he:

"Much, no doubt, can be said in favor of the justice and policy of a separation. It may be said that Secession or revolution in any of the United States would be subversive of all Federal authority, and, so far as the central Government is concerned, the resolving of the community into its original elements—that, if part of the States form new combinations and, Governments, other States may do the same. Then it may be said, why should not New York city, instead of supporting by her contributions in revenue two-thirds of the expenses of the United States, become also equally independent? As a Free City, with but nominal duty on imports, her local Government could be supported without taxation upon her people. Thus we could live free from taxes, and have cheap goods nearly duty free.

In this she would have the whole and united support of the Southern States, as well as all the other States to whose interests and rights under the Constitution she has always been true."

That is the persuasive casuistry peculiar to the minds of the Southern Secession leaders. It is naturally followed by a touch of that self-confident bluster, also at that time peculiar to Southern lips—as follows:

"It is well for individuals or communities to look every danger square in the face, and to meet it calmly and bravely. As dreadful as the severing of the bonds that have hitherto united the States has been in contemplation, it is now apparently a stern and inevitable fact. We have now to meet it, with all the consequences, whatever they may be. If the Confederacy is broken up the Government is dissolved, and it behooves every distinct community, as well as every individual, to take care of themselves.

"When Disunion has become a fixed and certain fact, why may not New York disrupt the bands which bind her to a venal and corrupt master—to a people and a Party that have plundered her revenues, attempted to ruin her commerce, taken away the power of self-government, and destroyed the Confederacy of which she was the proud Empire City? * * *"

After thus restating, as it were, the views and "arguments" of the Rebel Junta, as we may presume them to have been pressed on him, he becomes suddenly startled at the Conclave's idea of meeting "all the consequences, whatever they may be," and, turning completely around, with blanching pen, concludes:

"But I am not prepared to recommend the violence implied in these views. In stating this argument in favor of freedom, 'peaceably if we can, forcibly if we must,' let me not be misunderstood. The redress can be found only in appeals to the magnanimity of the people of the whole State." * * *

If "these views" were his own, and not those of the Rebel Conclave, he would either have been "prepared to recommend the violence implied in them," or else he would have suppressed them altogether. But his utterance is that of one who has certain views for the first time placed before him, and shrinks from the consequences of their advocacy—shrinks from "the violence implied" in them—although for some reason he dares not refuse to place those views before the people.

And, in carrying out his promise to do so—"In stating this argument," presumably of the Rebel Conclave, "in favor of freedom, 'peaceably if we can, forcibly if we must'"—the language used is an admission that the argument is not his own. Were it his own, would he not have said in "making" it, instead of in "stating" it? Furthermore, had he been "making" it of his own accord, he would hardly have involved himself in such singular contradictions and explanations as are here apparent. He was plainly "stating" the Rebel Conclave's argument, not making one himself. He was obeying orders, under the protest of his fears. And those fears forced his trembling pen to write the saving-clause which "qualifies" the Conclave's second-hand bluster preceding it.

That the Rebels hoped for Northern assistance in case of Secession, is very clear from many speeches made prior to and soon after the election of Mr. Lincoln to the Presidency—and from other sources of information. Thus we find in a speech made by Representative L. M. Keitt, of South Carolina, in Charleston, November, 1860, the following language, reported by the Mercury:

"But we have been threatened. Mr. Amos Kendall wrote a letter, in which he said to Colonel Orr, that if the State went out, three hundred thousand volunteers were ready to march against her. I know little about Kendall—and the less the better. He was under General Jackson; but for him the Federal treasury seemed to have a magnetic attraction.

"Jackson was a pure man, but he had too many around him who made fortunes far transcending their salaries. [Applause.] And this Amos Kendall had the same good fortune under Van Buren. He (Kendall) threatened us on the one side, and John Hickman on the other. John Hickman said, defiantly, that if we went out of the Union, eighteen millions of Northern men would bring us back.

"Let me tell you, there are a million of Democrats in the North who, when the Black Republicans attempt to march upon the South, will be found a wall of fire in the front. [Cries of 'that's so,' and applause.]"

Harper's Weekly of May 28, 1864, commenting on certain letters of M. F. Maury and others, then just come to light, said:

"How far Maury and his fellow-conspirators were justified in their hopes of seducing New Jersey into the Rebellion, may be gathered from the correspondence that took place, in the spring of 1861, between Ex-Governor Price, of New Jersey, who was one of the representatives from that State in the Peace Congress, and L. W. Burnet, Esq., of Newark.

"Mr. Price, in answering the question what ought New Jersey to do, says: 'I believe the Southern confederation permanent. The proceeding has been taken with forethought and deliberation—it is no hurried impulse, but an irrevocable act, based upon the sacred, as was supposed, equality of the States; and in my opinion every Slave State will in a short period of time be found united in one Confederacy. * * * Before that event happens, we cannot act, however much we may suffer in our material interests. It is in that contingency, then, that I answer the second part of your question:— What position for New Jersey will best accord with her interests, honor, and the patriotic instincts of her people? I say emphatically she would go with the South from every wise, prudential, and patriotic reason.'

"Ex-Governor Price proceeds to say that he is confident the States of Pennsylvania and New York will 'choose also to cast their lot with the South, and after them, the Western and Northwestern States.'"

The following resolution,* was adopted with others, by a meeting of Democrats held January 16, 1861, at National Hall, Philadelphia, and has been supposed to disclose "a plan, of which ex-Governor Price was likely aware:"

"Twelfth—That in the deliberate judgment of the Democracy of Philadelphia, and, so far as we know it, of Pennsylvania, the dissolution of the Union by the separation of the whole South, a result we shall most sincerely lament, may release this Commonwealth to a large extent from the bonds which now connect her with the Confederacy, except so far as for temporary convenience she chooses to submit to them, and would authorize and require her citizens, through a Convention, to be assembled for that purpose, to determine with whom her lot should be cast, whether with the North and the East, whose fanaticism has precipitated this misery upon us, or with our brethren of the South, whose wrongs we feel as our own; or whether Pennsylvania should stand by herself, as a distinct community, ready when occasion offers, to bind together the broken Union, and resume her place of loyalty and devotion."

Senator Lane of Oregon, replying to Senator Johnson of Tennessee, December 19, 1860, in the United States Senate, and speaking of and for the Northern Democracy, said:

"They will not march with him under his bloody banner, or Mr. Lincoln's, to invade the soil of the gallant State of South Carolina, when she may withdraw from a Confederacy that has refused her that equality to which she is entitled, as a member of the Union, under the Constitution. On the contrary, when he or any other gentleman raises that banner and attempts to subjugate that gallant people, instead of marching with him, we will meet him there, ready to repel him and his forces. He shall not bring with him the Northern Democracy to strike down a people contending for rights that have been refused them in a Union that ought to recognize the equality of every member of the Confederacy. * * * I now serve notice that, when War is made upon that gallant South for withdrawing from a Union which refuses them their rights, the Northern Democracy will not join in the crusade. THE REPUBLICAN PARTY WILL HAVE WAR ENOUGH AT HOME. THE DEMOCRACY OF THE NORTH NEED NOT CROSS THE BORDER TO FIND AN ENEMY."

The following letter from Ex-President Pierce is in the same misleading strain:

"CLARENDON HOTEL, January 6, 1860.—[This letter was captured, at Jeff. Davis's house in Mississippi, by the Union troops.]

"MY DEAR FRIEND:—I wrote you an unsatisfactory note a day or two since. I have just had a pleasant interview with Mr. Shepley, whose courage and fidelity are equal to his learning and talents. He says he would rather fight the battle with you as the standard-bearer in 1860, than under the auspices of any other leader. The feeling and judgment of Mr. S. in this relation is, I am confident, rapidly gaining ground in New England. Our people are looking for 'the coming man,' one who is raised by all the elements of his character above the atmosphere ordinarily breathed by politicians, a man really fitted for this exigency by his ability, courage, broad statesmanship, and patriotism. Colonel Seymour (Thomas H.) arrived here this morning, and expressed his views in this relation in almost the identical language used by Mr. Shepley.

"It is true that, in the present state of things at Washington and throughout the country, no man can predict what changes two or three months may bring forth. Let me suggest that, in the running debates in Congress, full justice seems to me not to have been done to the Democracy of the North. I do not believe that our friends at the South have any just idea of the state of feeling, hurrying at this moment to the pitch of intense exasperation, between those who respect their political obligations and those who have apparently no impelling power but that which fanatical passion on the subject of Domestic Slavery imparts.

"Without discussing the question of right, of abstract power to Secede, I have never believed that actual disruption of the Union can occur without blood; and if, through the madness of Northern Abolitionism, that dire calamity must come, THE FIGHTING WILL NOT BE ALONG MASON'S AND DIXON'S LINE MERELY. IT [WILL] BE WITHIN OUR OWN BORDERS, IN OUR OWN STREETS, BETWEEN THE TWO CLASSES OF CITIZENS TO WHOM I HAVE REFERRED. Those who defy law and scout Constitutional obligations will, if we ever reach the arbitrament of arms, FIND OCCUPATION ENOUGH AT HOME.

"Nothing but the state of Mrs. Pierce's health would induce me to leave the Country now, although it is quite likely that my presence at home would be of little service.

"I have tried to impress upon our people, especially in New Hampshire and Connecticut, where the only elections are to take place during the coming spring, that while our Union meetings are all in the right direction, and well enough for the present, they will not be worth the paper upon which their resolutions are written unless we can overthrow political Abolitionism at the polls and repeal the Unconstitutional and obnoxious laws which, in the cause of 'personal liberty,' have been placed upon our statute-books. I shall look with deep interest, and not without hope, for a decided change in this relation.

"Ever and truly your friend, "FRANKLIN PIERCE.

"Hon. JEFF. DAVIS, "Washington, D. C."

But let us turn from contemplating the encouragements to Southern Treason and Rebellion, held out by Northern Democratic Copperheads, to the more pleasing spectacle of Loyalty and Patriotism exhibited by the Douglas wing of Democracy.

Immediately after Sumter, and while the President was formulating his Message, calling for 75,000 volunteers, Douglas called upon him at the White House, regretted that Mr. Lincoln did not propose to call for thrice as many; and on the 18th of April, having again visited the White House, wrote, and gave the following dispatch to the Associated Press, for circulation throughout the Country:

"April 18, 1861, Senator Douglas called on the President, and had an interesting conversation on the present condition of the Country. The substance of it was, on the part of Mr. Douglas, that while he was unalterably opposed to the administration in all its political issues, he was prepared to fully sustain the President in the exercise of all his Constitutional functions, to preserve the Union, maintain the Government, and defend the Federal Capital. A firm policy and prompt action was necessary. The Capital was in danger and must be defended at all hazards, and at any expense of men and money. He spoke of the present and future without any reference to the past."

It is stated of this meeting and its immediate results: "The President was deeply gratified by the interview. To the West, Douglas telegraphed, 'I am for my Country and against all its assailants.' The fire of his patriotism spread to the masses of the North, and Democrat and Republican rallied to the support of the flag. In Illinois the Democratic and Republican presses vied with each other in the utterance of patriotic sentiments. * * * Large and numerously attended Mass meetings met, as it were with one accord, irrespective of parties, and the people of all shades of political opinions buried their party hatchets. Glowing and eloquent orators exhorted the people to ignore political differences in the present crisis, join in the common cause, and rally to the flag of the Union and the Constitution. It was a noble truce. From the many resolutions of that great outpouring of patriotic sentiment, which ignored all previous party ties, we subjoin the following:

"'Resolved, that it is the duty of all patriotic citizens of Illinois, without distinction of party or sect, to sustain the Government through the peril which now threatens the existence of the Union; and of our Legislature to grant such aid of men and money as the exigency of the hour and the patriotism of our people shall demand.'

"Governor Yates promptly issued his proclamation, dated the 15th of April, convening the Legislature for the 23rd inst. in Extraordinary Session.
* * * * * * *

"On the evening of the 25th of April, Mr. Douglas, who had arrived at the Capital the day before, addressed the General Assembly and a densely packed audience, in the Hall of Representatives, in that masterly effort, which must live and be enshrined in the hearts of his countrymen so long as our Government shall endure. Douglas had ever delighted in the mental conflicts of Party strife; but now, when his Country was assailed by the red hand of Treason, he was instantly divested of his Party armor and stood forth panoplied only in the pure garb of a true Patriot.

"He taught his auditory—he taught his Country, for his speeches were telegraphed all over it—the duty of patriotism at that perilous hour of the Nation's Life. He implored both Democrats and Republicans to lay aside their Party creeds and Platforms; to dispense with Party Organizations and Party Appeals; to forget that they were ever divided until they had first rescued the Government from its assailants. His arguments were clear, convincing, and unanswerable; his appeals for the Salvation of his Country, irresistible. It was the last speech, but one, he ever made."

Among other pithy and patriotic points made by him in that great speech —[July 9, 1861.]—were these: "So long as there was a hope of a peaceful solution, I prayed and implored for Compromise. I have spared no effort for a peaceful solution of these troubles; I have failed, and there is but one thing to do—to rally under the flag." "The South has no cause of complaint." "Shall we obey the laws or adopt the Mexican system of War, on every election." "Forget Party—all remember only your Country." "The shortest road to Peace is the most tremendous preparation for War." "It is with a sad heart and with a grief I have never before experienced, that I have to contemplate this fearful Struggle. * * * But it is our duty to protect the Government and the flag from every assailant, be he who he may."

In Chicago, Douglas repeated his patriotic appeal for the preservation of the Union, and tersely declared that "There can be no Neutrals in this War—only Patriots and Traitors." In that city he was taken with a mortal illness, and expired at the Tremont House, June 3, 1861—just one month prior to the meeting of the called Session of Congress.

The wonderful influence wielded by Douglas throughout the North, was well described afterward by his colleague, Judge Trumbull, in the Senate, when he said: "His course had much to do in producing that unanimity in support of the Government which is now seen throughout the Loyal States. The sublime spectacle of twenty million people rising as one man in vindication of Constitutional Liberty and Free Government, when assailed by misguided Rebels and plotting Traitors, is, to a considerable extent due to his efforts. His magnanimous and patriotic course in this trying hour of his Country's destiny was the crowning act of his life."

And Senator McDougall of California—his life-long friend—in describing the shock of the first intelligence that reached him, of his friend's sudden death, with words of even greater power, continued: "But, as, powerless for the moment to resist the tide of emotions, I bowed my head in silent grief, it came to me that the Senator had lived to witness the opening of the present unholy War upon our Government; that, witnessing it, from the Capital of his State, as his highest and best position, he had sent forth a War-cry worthy of that Douglass, who, as ancient legends tell, with the welcome of the knightly Andalusian King, was told,

"'Take thou the leading of the van, And charge the Moors amain; There is not such a lance as thine In all the hosts of Spain.'

"Those trumpet notes, with a continuous swell, are sounding still throughout all the borders of our Land. I heard them upon the mountains and in the valleys of the far State whence I come. They have communicated faith and strength to millions. * * * I ceased to grieve for Douglas. The last voice of the dead Douglas I felt to be stronger than the voice of multitudes of living men."

And here it may not be considered out of place for a brief reference to the writer's own position at this time; especially as it has been much misapprehended and misstated. One of the fairest of these statements* runs thus:

[Lusk's History of the Politics of Illinois from 1856 to 1884, p. 175.]

"It is said that Logan did not approve the great speech made by Senator Douglas, at Springfield, in April, 1861, wherein he took the bold ground that in the contest which was then clearly imminent to him, between the North and the South, that there could be but two parties, Patriots and Traitors. But granting that there was a difference between Douglas and Logan at that time, it did not relate to their adhesion to the Cause of their Country Logan had fought for the Union upon the plains of Mexico, and again stood ready to give his life, if need be, for his Country, even amid the cowardly slanders that were then following his pathway.

"The difference between Douglas and Logan was this: Mr. Douglas was fresh from an extended campaign in the dissatisfied Sections of the Southern States, and he was fully apprised of their intention to attempt the overthrow of the Union, and was therefore in favor of the most stupendous preparations for War.

"Mr. Logan, on the other hand, believed in exhausting all peaceable means before a resort to Arms, and in this he was like President Lincoln; but when he saw there was no alternative but to fight, he was ready and willing for armed resistance, and, resigning his seat in Congress, entered the Army, as Colonel of the Thirty-first Illinois Infantry, and remained in the field in active service until Peace was declared."

This statement is, in the main, both fair and correct.

It is no more correct, however, in intimating that "Logan did not approve the great speech made by Senator Douglas, at Springfield, in April, 1861, wherein he took the bold ground that in the contest which was then clearly imminent to him, between the North and the South, that there could be but two parties, Patriots and Traitors," than others have been in intimating that he was disloyal to the Union, prior to the breaking out of hostilities—a charge which was laid out flat in the Senate Chamber, April 19, 1881.

[In Dawson's Life of Logan, pp. 348-353, this matter is thus alluded to:

"In an early part of this work the base charge that Logan was not loyal before the War has been briefly touched on. It may be well here to touch on it more fully. As was then remarked, the only man that ever dared insinuate to Logan's face that he was a Secession sympathizer before the War, was Senator Ben Hill of Georgia, in the United States Senate Chamber, March 30, 1881; and Logan instantly retorted: 'Any man who insinuates that I sympathized with it at that time insinuates what is false,' and Senator Hill at once retracted the insinuation."

"Subsequently, April 19, 1881, Senator Logan, in a speech, fortified with indisputable record and documentary evidence, forever set at rest the atrocious calumny. From that record it appears that on the 17th December, 1860, while still a Douglas Democrat, immediately after Lincoln's election, and long before his inauguration, and before even the first gun of the war was fired, Mr. Logan, then a Representative in the House, voted affirmatively on a resolution, offered by Morris of Illinois, which declared an 'immovable attachment' to 'our National Union,' and 'that it is our patriotic duty to stand by it as our hope in peace and our defense in war;' that on the 7th January, 1861, Mr. Adrian having offered the following 'Resolved, That we fully approve of the bold and patriotic act of Major Anderson in withdrawing from Fort Moultrie to Fort Sumter, and of the determination of the President to maintain that fearless officer in his present position; and that we will support the President in all constitutional measures to enforce the laws and preserve the Union'—Mr. Logan, in casting his vote, said: 'As the resolution receives my unqualified approval, I vote Aye;' and that further on the 5th of February, 1861, before the inauguration of President Lincoln, in a speech made by Logan in the House in favor of the Crittenden Compromise measures, he used the following language touching Secession:

"'Sir, I have always denied, and do yet deny, the right of Secession. There is no warrant for it in the Constitution. It is wrong, it is unlawful, unconstitutional, and should be called by the right name—revolution. No good, sir, can result from it, but much mischief may. It is no remedy for any grievances. I hold that all grievances can be much easier redressed inside the Union than out of it.'

"In that same speech he also * * * said:

"'I have been taught that the preservation of this glorious Union, with its broad flag waving over us as the shield for our protection on land and on sea, is paramount to all the parties and platforms that ever have existed or ever can exist. I would, to day, if I had the power, sink my own party and every other one, with all their platforms, into the vortex of ruin, without heaving a sigh or shedding a tear, to save the Union, or even stop the revolution where it is.'

"In this most complete speech of vindication—which Senator Logan said he put upon record, 'First, that my children, after me, may not have these slanders thrown in their faces without the power of dispelling or refuting them; and second, that they may endure in this Senate Chamber, so that it may be a notice to Senators of all parties and all creeds that hereafter, while I am here in the Senate, no insinuation of that kind will be submitted to by me'—the proofs of the falsity of the charge were piled mountain-high, and among them the following voluntary statements from two Democratic Senators, who were with him before the War, in the House of Representatives:

"'United States Senate Chamber, WASHINGTON, April 14, 1881.

"'DEAR SIR: In a discussion in the Senate a few weeks since you referred to the fact that a Southern Senator, who had served with you in Congress before the War, could testify that during your term of service there you gave no encouragement to the Secession of the Southern States, adding, however, that you did not ask such testimony. I was not sure at the time that your reference was to me, as Senator Pugh of Alabama, was also a member of that Congress.

"'Since then, having learned that your reference was to me, I propose on the floor of the Senate, should suitable occasion offer, to state what I know of your position and views at the time referred to. But, as I may be absent from the Senate for some time, I deem it best to give you this written statement, with full authority to use it in any way that seems proper to you.

"'When you first came to Congress in——, you were a very ardent and impetuous Democrat. In the division which took place between Mr. Douglas and his friends, on the one hand, and the Southern Democrats, on the other, you were a warm and uncompromising supporter of Mr. Douglas; and in the course of that convention you became somewhat estranged from your party associates in the South. In our frequent discussions upon the subjects of difference, I never heard a word of sympathy from your lips with Secession in either theory or practice. On the contrary, you were vehement in your opposition to it.'

"'I remember well a conversation I had with you just before leaving Washington to become a candidate for the Secession convention. You expressed the deep regret you felt at my proposed action, and deplored the contemplated movement in terms as strong as any I heard from any Republican.' Yours truly, "'L. Q. C. LAMAR

"'Hon. JOHN A. LOGAN. "United States Senate, Washington, D. C.'

"Senate Chamber, April 14, 1881.

"'Having read the above statement of Senator Lamar, I fully concur with him in my recollection of your expressions and action in opposition to

Secession. Truly yours, J. L. PUGH.'

"At the conclusion of Senator Logan's speech of refutation, Senator Brown of Georgia (Democrat) said:

"'Our newspapers may have misrepresented his position. I am now satisfied they did. I have heard the Senator's statement with great interest, and I take pleasure in saying—for I had some idea before that there was some shadow of truth in this report—that I think his vindication' is full, complete, and conclusive.'

"'I recollect very well during the war, when I was Governor of my State and the Federal army was invading it, to have had a large force of militia aiding the Confederate army, and that Gen. Logan was considered by us as one of the ablest, most gallant, and skillful leaders of the Federal army. We had occasion to feel his power, and we learned to respect him.'

"Senator Beck, of Kentucky (Democrat), referring to the fact that he was kept out of the House at one time, and a great many suggestions had been made to him as to General Logan, continued:

"'As I said the other day, I never proposed to go into such things, and never have done so; but at that time General Frank Blair was here, and I submitted many of the papers I received to him,—I never thought of using any of them,—and I remember the remark that he made to me: Beck, John Logan was one of the hardest fighters of the war; and when many men who were seeking to whistle him down the wind because of his politics when the war began, were snugly fixed in safe places, he was taking his life in his hand wherever the danger was greatest—and I tore up every paper I got, and burnt it in the fire before his eyes.'

"Senator Dawes of Massachusetts (Republican), also took occasion to say:

"Mr. President, I do not know that anything which can be said on this side would be of any consequence to the Senator from Illinois in this matter. But I came into the House of Representatives at the same session that the Senator did.

"'He was at that time one of the most intense of Democrats, and I was there with him when the Rebellion first took root and manifested itself in open and flagrant war; and I wish to say as a Republican of that day, when the Senator from Illinois was a Democrat, that at the earliest possible moment when the Republican Party was in anxiety as to the position of the Northern Democracy on the question of forcible assault on the Union, nothing did they hail with more delight than the early stand which the Senator from Illinois, from the Democratic side of the House, took upon the question of resistance to the Government of the United States.

"I feel that it is right that I should state that he was among the first, if not the very first, of the Northern Democrats who came out openly and declared, whatever may have been their opinion about the doctrines of the Republican Party, that when it came to a question of forcible resistance, they should be counted on the side of the Government, and in co-operation with the Republican Party in the attempt to maintain its authority.'

"'I am very glad, whether it be of any service or not, to bear this testimony to the early stand the Senator from Illinois took while he was still a Democrat, and the large influence he exerted upon the Northern Democracy, which kept it from being involved in the condition and in the work of the Southern Democracy at that time.'"]

So far from this being the case, the fact is—and it is here mentioned in part to bring out the interesting point that, had he lived, Douglas would have been no idle spectator of the great War that was about to be waged—that when Douglas visited Springfield, Illinois, to make that great speech in the latter part of April, 1861, the writer went there also, to see and talk over with him the grave situation of affairs, not only in the Nation generally, but particularly in Illinois. And on that occasion Mr. Douglas said to him, substantially: "The time has now arrived when a man must be either for or against his Country. Indeed so strongly do I feel this, and that further dalliance with this question is useless, that I shall myself take steps to join the Array, and fight for the maintenance of the Union."

To this the writer replied that he was "equally well convinced that each and every man must take his stand," and that he also "purposed at an early day to raise a Regiment and draw the sword in that Union's defense."

This was after Sumter, and only seventy days before Congress was to meet in Called Session. When that session met, Douglas had, weeks before, gone down to the grave amid the tears of a distracted Nation, with the solemn injunction upon his dying lips: "Obey the Laws and Defend the Constitution"—and the writer had returned to Washington, to take his seat in Congress, with that determination still alive in his heart.

In fact there had been all along, substantial accord between Mr. Douglas and the writer. There really was no "difference between Douglas and Logan" as to "preparations for War," or in "exhausting all Peaceable means before a resort to Arms," and both were in full accord with President Lincoln on these points.

Let us see if this is not of record: Take the writer's speech in the House of Representatives, February 5, 1861, and it will be seen that he said: "I will go as far as any man in the performance of a Constitutional duty to put down Rebellion, to suppress Insurrection, and to enforce the Laws." Again, he said, "If all the evils and calamities that have ever happened since the World began, could be gathered in one Great Catastrophe, its horrors could not eclipse, in their frightful proportions, the Drama that impends over us."

From these extracts it is plain enough that even at this very early day the writer fully understood the "frightful proportions" of the impending struggle, and would "go as far as"—not only Mr. Douglas, but—"any man, to put down Rebellion"—which necessarily involved War, and "preparations for War." But none the less, but rather the more, because of the horrors which he foresaw must be inseparable from so terrible a War, was he anxious by timely mutual Concessions—"by any sacrifice," as he termed it—if possible, to avert it.

He was ready to sink Party, self, and to accept any of the Propositions to that end—Mr. Douglas's among them.

[See his speech of February 5, 1861, Congressional Globe]

In this attitude also he was in accord with Mr. Douglas, who, as well as the writer, was ready to make any sacrifice, of Party or self; to "exhaust every effort at peaceful adjustment," before resorting to War. The fact is they were much of the time in consultation, and always in substantial accord.

In a speech made in the Senate, March 15, 1861, Mr. Douglas had reduced the situation to the following three alternative points:

"1. THE RESTORATION AND PRESERVATION OF THE UNION by such Amendments to the Constitution as will insure the domestic tranquillity, safety, and equality of all the States, and thus restore peace, unity, and fraternity, to the whole Country.

"2. A PEACEFUL DISSOLUTION OF THE UNION by recognizing the Independence of such States as refuse to remain in the Union without such Constitutional Amendments, and the establishment of a liberal system of commercial and social intercourse with them by treaties of commerce and amity.

"3. WAR, with a view to the subjugation and military occupation of those States which have Seceded or may Secede from the Union."

As a thorough Union man, he could never have agreed to a "Peaceful Dissolution of the Union." On the other hand he was equally averse to War, because he held that "War is Disunion. War is final, eternal Separation." Hence, all his energies and talents were given to carrying out his first-stated line of policy, and to persuading the Seceders to accept what in that line was offered to them by the dominant party.

His speech in the Senate, March 25, 1861, was a remarkable effort in that respect. Mr. Breckinridge had previously spoken, and had declared that: "Whatever settlement may be made of other questions, this must be settled upon terms that will give them [the Southern States] either a right, in common with others, to emigrate into all the territory, or will secure to them their rights on a principle of equitable division."

Mr. Douglas replied: "Now, under the laws as they stand, in every Territory of the United States, without any exception, a Southern man can go with his Slave-property on equal terms with all other property. * * * Every man, either from the North or South, may go into the Territories with his property on terms of exact equality, subject to the local law; and Slave-property stands on an equal footing with all other kinds of property in the Territories of the United States. It now stands on an equal footing in all the

Territories for the first time.

"I have shown you that, up to 1859, little more than a year ago, it was prohibited in part of the Territories. It is not prohibited anywhere now. For the first time, under Republican rule, the Southern States have secured that equality of rights in the Territories for their Slave-property which they have been demanding so long."

He held that the doctrine of Congressional prohibition in all the Territories, as incorporated in the Wilmot proviso, had now been repudiated by the Republicans of both Houses of Congress, who had "all come over to Non-intervention and Popular Sovereignty;" that the "Wilmot proviso is given up; that Congressional prohibition is given up; that the aggressive policy is repudiated; and hereafter the Southern man and the Northern man may move into the Territories with their Property on terms of entire equality, without excepting Slaves or any other kind of property."

Continuing, he said: "What more do the Southern States want? What more can any man demand? Non-intervention is all you asked. Will it be said the South required in addition to this, laws of Congress to protect Slavery in the Territories? That cannot be said; for only last May, the Senate, by a nearly unanimous vote—a unanimous vote of the Southern men, with one or two exceptions—declared that affirmative legislation was not needed at this time. * * * What cause is there for further alarm in the Southern States, so far as the Territories are concerned? * * *

"I repeat, the South has got all they ever claimed in all the Territories. * * * Then, sir, according to law, the Slaveholding States have got equality in the Territories. How is it in fact. * * * Now, I propose to show that they have got the actual equitable partition, giving them more than they were disposed to demand.

"The Senator from Kentucky, * * * Mr. Crittenden, introduced a proposition for an equitable partition. That proposition was, that north of 36 30' Slavery should be prohibited, and South of it should be protected, by Territorial law. * * * What is now the case? It is true the Crittenden proposition has not yet become part of the Constitution; but it is also true that an equitable partition has been made by the vote of the people themselves, establishing, maintaining, and protecting Slavery in every inch of territory South of the thirty-seventh parallel, giving the South half a degree more than the Crittenden Proposition.

"There stands your Slave-code in New Mexico protecting Slavery up to the thirty-seventh degree as effectually as laws can be made to protect it. There it stands the Law of the Land. Therefore the South has all below the thirty-seventh parallel, while Congress has not prohibited Slavery even North of it.

* * * * * *

"What more, then, is demanded? Simply that a Constitutional Amendment

48

shall be adopted, affirming—what? Precisely what every Republican in both Houses of Congress has voted for within a month. Just do, by Constitutional Amendment, what you have voted in the Senate and House of Representatives, that is all. You are not even required to do that, but merely to vote for a proposition submitting the question to the People of the States whether they will make a Constitutional Amendment affirming the equitable partition of the Territories which the People have already made. * * *

"You may ask, why does the South want us to do it by Constitutional Amendment, when we have just done it voluntarily by Law? The President of the United States, in his Inaugural, has told you the reason. He has informed you that all of these troubles grow out of the absence of a Constitutional provision defining the power of Congress over the subject of Slavery. * * * He thinks that the trouble has arisen from the absence of such a Constitutional Provision, and suggests a National Convention to enable the People to supply the defect, leaving the People to say what it is, instead of dictating to them what it shall be."

It may here be remarked that while Mr. Douglas held that "So far as the doctrine of Popular Sovereignty and Nonintervention is concerned, the Colorado Bill, the Nevada Bill, and the Dakota Bill, are identically the same with the Kansas-Nebraska Bill, and in its precise language"—these former Bills having been passed at the last Session of the 36th Congress—the Republicans, on the contrary, held that neither in these nor other measures had they abandoned any distinctive Republican principle; while Breckinridge declared that they had passed those Territorial Bills, without the Wilmot proviso, because they felt perfectly secure in those Territories, with all the Federal patronage in Republican hands.

However that may be, we have here, brought out in strong contrast, the conciliatory feeling which inspired such Union men as Douglas, and the strong and persistent efforts they made in behalf of Concession and Peace up to a period only a few weeks before the bombardment of Sumter; and the almost total revulsion in their sentiments after that event, as to the only proper means to preserve the Union. For it was only then that the truth, as it fell from Douglas's lips at Springfield, was fully recognized, to wit: that there was no half-way ground betwixt Patriotism and Treason; that War was an existing fact; and that Patriots must arm to defend and preserve the Union against the armed Traitors assailing it.

At last, July 4, 1861, the Congress met, and proceeded at once with commendable alacrity and patriotism, to the consideration and enactment of measures sufficient to meet the extraordinary exigency, whether as regards the raising and equipment of the vast bodies of Union volunteers needed to put down Rebellion, or in the raising of those enormous amounts of money which the Government was now, or might thereafter be, called upon to spend like water in preserving the Union.

It was at this memorable Session, of little over one month, that the chief of the great "War Measures" as they were termed, were enacted.

THE STORM OF BATTLE

We have seen how Fort Sumter fell; how the patriotic North responded to President Lincoln's Call, for 75,000 three-months volunteers, with such enthusiasm that, had there been a sufficiency of arms and accoutrements, he might have had, within three months of that Call, an Army of 500,000 men in the field; how he had called for 42,000 three-years volunteers early in May, besides swelling what little there was of a regular Army by ten full regiments; and how a strict blockade of the entire Southern Coast-line had not only been declared, but was now enforced and respected.

General Butler, promoted Major-General for his Military successes at Annapolis and Baltimore, was now in command of Fortress Monroe and vicinity, with some 12,000 volunteers under him, confronted, on the Peninsula, by a nearly equal number of Rebel troops, under Generals Huger and Magruder—General Banks, with less than 10,000 Union troops, occupying Baltimore, and its vicinage.

General Patterson, with some 20,000 Union troops—mostly Pennsylvania militia—was at Chambersburg, Pennsylvania, with about an equal number of the Enemy, under General Joseph E. Johnston, at Harper's Ferry, on the Potomac, watching him.

Some 50,000 Union troops were in camp, in and about Washington, on the Virginia side, under the immediate command of Generals McDowell and Mansfield—Lieutenant General Scott, at Washington, being in Chief-command of the Union Armies—and, confronting these Union forces, in Virginia, near the National Capital, were some 30,000 Rebel troops under the command of General Beauregard, whose success in securing the evacuation of Fort Sumter by its little garrison of half-starved Union soldiers, had magnified him, in the eyes of the rebellious South, into the proportions of a Military genius of the first order.

There had been no fighting, nor movements, worthy of special note, until June 7th, when General Patterson advanced from Chambersburg, Pennsylvania, to Hagerstown, Maryland. General Johnston at once evacuated Harper's Ferry, and retreated upon Winchester, Virginia.

General McClellan, in command of the Department of the Ohio, had, however, crossed the Ohio river, and by the 4th of July, being at Grafton, West Virginia, with his small Army of Union troops, to which a greatly inferior Rebel force was opposed, commenced that successful advance against it, which led, after Bull Run, to his being placed at the head of all the Armies of the United States.

Subsequently Patterson crossed the Potomac, and after trifling away over one month's time, at last, on the 15th of July, got within nine miles of Winchester and Johnston's Army. Barring a spiritless reconnaissance, Patterson—who was a fervent Breckinridge-Democrat in politics, and whose Military judgment, as we shall see, was greatly influenced, if not entirely controlled, by his Chief of staff, Fitz John Porter—never got any nearer to the Enemy!

Instead of attacking the Rebel force, under Johnston, or at least keeping it "employed," as he was ordered to do by General Scott; instead of getting nearer, and attempting to get between Winchester and the Shenandoah River, as was suggested to him by his second in command, General Sanford; and instead of permitting Sanford to go ahead, as that General desired to, with his own 8,000 men, and do it himself; General Patterson ordered him off to Charlestown—twelve miles to the Union left and rear,—and then took the balance of his Army, with himself, to the same place!

In other words, while he had the most positive and definite orders, from General Scott, if not to attack and whip Johnston, to at least keep him busy and prevent that Rebel General from forming a junction, via the Manassas Gap railroad or otherwise, with Beauregard, Patterson deliberately moved his Army further away from Winchester and gave to the Enemy the very chance of escaping and forming that junction which was essential to Rebel success in the vicinity of Manassas.

But for this disobedience of orders, Bull Run would doubtless have been a great victory to the Union Arms, instead of a reverse, and the War, which afterward lasted four years, might have been over in as many months.

It is foreign to the design of this work, to present in it detailed descriptions of the battles waged during the great War of the Rebellion —it being the present intention of the writer, at some later day, to prepare and publish another work devoted to such stirring Military scenes. Yet, as it might seem strange and unaccountable for him to pass by, at this time, without any description or comment, the first pitched battle of the Rebellion, he is constrained to pause and view that memorable contest. And first, it may be well to say a word of the general topography of the country about the battle-field.

The Alleghany Mountains, or that part of them with which we have now to do, stretch in three almost equidistant parallel ridges, from North-East to South-West, through the heart of Old Virginia. An occasional pass, or "Gap," through these ridges, affords communication, by good roads, between the enclosed parallel valleys and the Eastern part of that State.

The Western of these Alleghany ridges bears the name of "Alleghany Mountains" proper; the Eastern is called the "Blue Ridge;" while the Middle Ridge, at its Northern end—which rests upon the Potomac, where that river sweeps through three parallel ridges almost at right angles to their own line of direction—is called the "Great North Mountain."

The valley, between the Middle Ridge and the Blue Ridge, is known as the Shenandoah Valley, taking its name from the Shenandoah River, which, for more than one hundred miles, flows along the Western foot of the Blue Ridge, toward the North-East, until it empties into the Potomac, at Harper's Ferry.

The Orange and Alexandria railroad runs from Alexandria,—on the opposite bank of the Potomac from Washington, and a few miles below the Capital,—in a general Southeasterly direction, to Culpepper Court-House; thence Southerly to Gordonsville, where it joins the Virginia Central—the Western branch of which runs thence through Charlotteville, Staunton, and Covington, across the ridges and valleys of the Alleghanies, while its Eastern branch, taking a general South-easterly direction, crosses the Richmond and Fredricksburg railroad at Hanover Junction, some twenty miles North of Richmond, and thence sweeps Southerly to the Rebel capital.

It is along this Easterly branch of the Virginia Central that Rebel re-enforcements will be hurried to Beauregard, from Richmond to Gordonsville, and thence, by the Orange and Alexandria railroad, to Manassas Junction.

Some twenty-five miles from Alexandria, a short railroad-feeder—which runs from Strasburg, in the Shenandoah Valley, through the Blue Ridge, at Manassas Gap, in an East-South-easterly direction—strikes the Alexandria and Orange railroad. The point of contact is Manassas Junction; and it is along this Manassas-Gap feeder that Johnston, with his Army at Winchester—some twenty miles North-North-East of Strasburg—expects, in case of attack by Patterson, to be re-enforced by Beauregard; or, in case the latter is assailed, to go to his assistance, after shaking off Patterson.

This little link of railroad, known as the Manassas Gap railroad, is therefore an important factor in the game of War, now commencing in earnest; and it had, as we shall see, very much to do, not only with the advance of McDowell's Union Army upon Bull Run, but also with the result of the first pitched battle thereabout fought.

From Alexandria, some twelve miles to the Westward, runs a fine turnpike road to Fairfax Court-House; thence, continuing Westward, but gradually and slightly dipping award the South, it passes through Germantown, Centreville, and Groveton, to Warrenton.

This "Warrenton Pike"—as it is termed—also plays a somewhat conspicuous part, before, during, and after the Battle of Bull Run. For most of its length, from Fairfax Court-House to Warrenton, the Warrenton Pike pursues a course almost parallel with the Orange and Alexandria railroad aforesaid, while the stream of Bull Run, pursuing a South-easterly course, has a general direction almost parallel with that of the Manassas Gap railroad.

We shall find that it is the diamond-shaped parallelogram, formed by the obtuse angle junction of the two railroads on the South, and the similarly obtuse-angled crossing of the stream of Bull Run by the Warrenton Pike on the North, that is destined to become the historic battle-field of the first "Bull Run," or "Manassas;" and it is in the Northern obtuse-angle of this parallelogram that the main fighting is done, upon a spot not much more than one mile square, three sides of the same being bounded respectively by the Bull Run stream, the Warrenton Pike, which crosses it on a stone bridge, and the Sudley Springs road, which crosses the Pike, at right-angles to it, near a stone house.

On the 3rd of June, 1861, General McDowell, in command of the Department of North-Eastern Virginia, with head-quarters at Arlington, near Washington, receives from Colonel Townsend, Assistant Adjutant-General with Lieutenant-General Scott—who is in Chief command of all the Union Forces, with Headquarters at Washington—a brief but pregnant communication, the body of which runs thus: "General Scott desires you to submit an estimate of the number and composition of a column to be pushed toward Manassas Junction, and perhaps the Gap, say in four or five days, to favor Patterson's attack on Harper's Ferry. The rumor is that Arlington Heights will be attacked to-night."

In response to this request, General McDowell submits, on the day following, an estimate that "the actual entire force at the head of the column should, for the purpose of carrying the position at Manassas and of occupying both the road to Culpepper, and the one to the Gap, be as much as 12,000 Infantry, two batteries of regular Artillery, and from six to eight companies of Cavalry, with an available reserve, ready to move forward from Alexandria by rail, of 5,000 Infantry and one heavy field battery, rifled if possible; these numbers to be increased or diminished as events may indicate." This force of raw troops he proposes to organize into field brigades under the command of "active and experienced colonels" of the regular Army. And while giving this estimate as to the number of troops necessary, he suggestively adds that "in proportion to the numbers used will be the lives saved; and as we have such numbers pressing to be allowed to serve, might it not be well to overwhelm and conquer as much by the show of force as by the use of it?"

Subsequently McDowell presents to General Scott, and Mr. Lincoln's Cabinet, a project of advance and attack, which is duly approved and ordered to be put in execution. In that project or plan of operations, submitted by verbal request of General Scott, near the end of June,—the success of which is made contingent upon Patterson's holding Johnston engaged at Winchester in the Shenandoah Valley, and also upon Butler's holding the Rebel force near Fortress Monroe from coming to Beauregard's aid at Manassas Junction,—McDowell estimates Beauregard's strength at 25,000, with a possible increase, bringing it up to 35,000 men. The objective point in McDowell's plan, is Manassas Junction, and he proposes "to move against Manassas with a force of 30,000 of all arms, organized into three columns, with a reserve of 10,000."

McDowell is fully aware that the Enemy has "batteries in position at several places in his front, and defensive works on Bull Run, and Manassas Junction." These batteries he proposes to turn. He believes Bull Run to be "fordable at almost anyplace,"—an error which ultimately renders his plan abortive,—and his proposition is, after uniting his columns on the Eastern side of Bull Run, "to attack the main position by turning it, if possible, so as to cut off communications by rail with the South, or threaten to do so sufficiently to force the Enemy to leave his intrenchments to guard them."

In other words, assuming the Enemy driven back, by minor flanking movements, or otherwise, upon his intrenched position at Bull Run, or Manassas, the plan is to turn his right, destroy the Orange and Alexandria railroad leading South, and the bridge at Bristol, so as to cut off his supplies. This done, the Enemy—if nothing worse ensues for him—will be in a "bad box."

McDowell, however, has no idea that the Enemy will stand still to let this thing be done. On the contrary, he is well satisfied that Beauregard will accept battle on some chosen ground between Manassas Junction and Washington.

On the afternoon of Tuesday, the 16th of July, the advance of McDowell's Army commences. That Army is organized into five divisions—four of which accompany McDowell, while a fifth is left to protect the defensive works of Washington, on the South bank of the Potomac. This latter, the Fourth Division, commanded by Brigadier-General Theodore Runyon, comprises eight unbrigaded New Jersey regiments of (three months, and three years) volunteers—none of which take part in the ensuing conflicts-at-arms.

The moving column consists of the First Division, commanded by

Brigadier-General Daniel Tyler, comprising four brigades, respectively under Brigadier-General R. C. Schenck, and Colonels E. D. Keyes, W. T. Sherman, and I. B. Richardson; the Second Division, commanded by Colonel David Hunter, comprising two brigades, under Colonels Andrew Porter and A. E. Burnside respectively; the Third Division, commanded by Colonel S. P. Heintzelman, comprising three brigades, under Colonels W. B. Franklin, O. B. Wilcox, and O. O. Howard, respectively; and the Fifth Division, commanded by Colonel Dixon S. Miles, comprising two brigades, under Colonels Lewis Blenker, and Thomas A. Davies, respectively.

Tyler's Division leads the advance, moving along the Leesburg road to Vienna, on our right, with orders to cross sharply to its left, upon Fairfax Court House, the following (Wednesday) morning. Miles's Division follows the turnpike road to Annandale, and then moves, by the Braddock road,—along which Braddock, a century before, had marched his doomed army to disaster,—upon Fairfax Court House, then known to be held by Bonham's Rebel Brigade of South Carolinians. Hunter follows Miles, to Annandale, and thence advances direct upon Fairfax, by the turnpike road—McDowell's idea being to bag Bonham's Brigade, if possible, by a simultaneous attack on the front and both flanks. But the advance is too slow, and the Enemy's outposts, both there and elsewhere, have ample opportunity of falling safely back upon their main position, behind the stream of Bull Run.

[McDowell in his testimony before the "Committee on the Conduct of the War," said: "At Fairfax Court House was the South Carolina Brigade. And I do not suppose anything would have had a greater cheering effect upon the troops, and perhaps upon the Country, than the capture of that brigade. And if General Tyler could have got down there any time in the forenoon instead of in the afternoon, the capture of that brigade was beyond question. It was about 5,000 or 6,000 men, and Tyler had 12,000, at the same time that we were pressing on in front. He did not get down there until in the afternoon; none of us got forward in time."]

This slowness is due to various causes. There is a pretty general dread, for example, among our troops, of threatened ambuscades, and hence the advance is more cautious than it otherwise would be. It is thought the part of wisdom, as it were, to "feel the way." The marching, moreover, is new to our troops. General Scott had checked McDowell when the latter undertook to handle eight regiments together, near Washington, by intimating that he was "trying to make a show." Thus the very essential knowledge of how to manoeuvre troops in large bodies, has been withheld from our Union generals, while the volunteer regiments have either rusted in camp from inaction, or have been denied the opportunity of acquiring that endurance and hardiness and discipline which frequent movement of troops confers. Hence, all unused to the discipline of the march, every moment some one falls out of line to "pick blackberries, or to get water." Says McDowell, in afterward reporting this march: "They would not keep in the ranks, order as much as you pleased. When they came where water was fresh, they would pour the old water out of their canteens and fill them with fresh water; they were not used to denying themselves much."

Meantime, Heintzelman's Division is also advancing, by cross-roads, more to the left and South of the railroad line,—in accordance with McDowell's plan, which comprehends not only the bagging of Bonham, but an immediate subsequent demonstration, by Tyler, upon Centreville and beyond, while Heintzelman, supported by Hunter and Miles, shall swoop across Bull Run, at Wolf Run Shoals, some distance below Union Mills, turn the Enemy's right, and cut off his Southern line of railroad communications. Thus, by the evening of Wednesday, the 17th, Heintzelman is at Sangster's Station, while Tyler, Miles, and Hunter, are at Fairfax.

It is a rather rough experience that now befalls the Grand Army of the Union. All unused, as we have seen, to the fatigues and other hardships of the march, the raw levies, of which it almost wholly consists, which started bright and fresh, strong and hopeful, full of the buoyant ardor of enthusiastic patriotism, on that hot July afternoon, only some thirty hours back, are now dust-begrimed, footsore, broken down, exhausted by the scorching sun, hungry, and without food,—for they have wasted the rations with which they started, and the supply-trains have not yet arrived. Thus, hungry and physically prostrated, "utterly played out," as many of them confess, and demoralized also by straggling and loss of organization, they bivouac that night in the woods, and dream uneasy dreams beneath the comfortless stars.

A mile beyond Fairfax Court House, on the Warrenton Turnpike, is Germantown. It is here that Tyler's Division has rested, on the night of the 17th. At 7 o'clock on the morning of Thursday, the 18th, in obedience to written orders from McDowell, it presses forward, on that "Pike," to Centreville, five miles nearer to the Enemy's position behind Bull Run— Richardson's Brigade in advance—and, at 9 o'clock, occupies it. Here McDowell has intended Tyler to remain, in accordance with the plan, which he has imparted to him in conversation, and in obedience to the written instructions to: "Observe well the roads to Bull Run and to Warrenton. Do not bring on an engagement, but keep up the impression that we are moving on Manassas,"—this advance, by way of Centreville, being intended solely as a "demonstration" to mask the real movement, which, as we have seen, is to be made by the other divisions across Wolf Run Shoals, a point on Bull Run, some five or six miles below Union Mills, and some seven miles below Blackburn's Ford.

Upon the arrival of Richardson's Brigade, Thursday morning, at Centreville, it is found that, under cover of the darkness of the previous night, the Enemy has retreated, in two bodies, upon Bull Run, the one along the Warrenton Pike, the other (the largest) down the ridge-road from Centreville to Blackburn's Ford. Richardson's Brigade at once turns down the latter road and halts about a mile beyond Centreville, at a point convenient to some springs of water. Tyler soon afterward rides up, and, taking from that brigade two companies of light Infantry and a squadron of Cavalry, proceeds, with Colonel Richardson, to reconnoitre the Enemy, finding him in a strong position on the opposite bank of Bull Run, at Blackburn's Ford.

While this is going on, McDowell has ridden in a Southerly direction down to Heintzelman's Division, at Sangster's Station, "to make arrangements to turn the Enemy's right, and intercept his communications with the South," but has found, owing to the narrowness and crookedness of the roads, and the great distance that must be traversed in making the necessary detour, that his contemplated movement is too risky to be ventured. Hence he at once abandons his original plan of turning the Enemy's right, and determines on "going around his left, where the country is more open, and the roads broad and good."

McDowell now orders a concentration, for that night, of the four divisions, with two days cooked rations in their haversacks, upon and about Centreville,—the movement to commence as soon as they shall receive expected commissariat supplies. But, later on the 18th,—learning that his advance, under Tyler, has, against orders, become engaged with the Enemy—he directs the concentration to be made at once.

Let us examine, for a moment, how this premature engagement comes about. We left Tyler, accompanied by Richardson, with a squadron of Cavalry and a battalion of light Infantry making a reconnaissance, on Thursday morning the 18th, toward Blackburn's Ford. They approach within a mile of the ford, when they discover a Rebel battery on the farther bank of Bull Run—so placed as to enfilade the road descending from their own position of observation down to the ford,—strong Rebel infantry pickets and skirmishing parties being in front.

Tyler at once orders up his two rifled guns, Ayres' Battery, and Richardson's entire Brigade—and later, Sherman's Brigade as a reserve. As soon as they come up,—about noon—he orders the rifled guns into battery on the crest of the hill, about one mile from, and looking down upon, the Rebel battery aforesaid, and opens upon the Enemy; giving him a dozen shells,—one of them making it lively for a body of Rebel Cavalry which appears between the ford and Manassas.

The Rebel battery responds with half a dozen shots, and then ceases. Tyler now orders Richardson to advance his brigade and throw out skirmishers to scour the thick woods which cover the Bull Run bottom-land. Richardson at once rapidly deploys the battalion of light Infantry as skirmishers in advance of his brigade, pushes them forward to the edge of the woods, drives in the skirmishers of the Enemy in fine style, and supports their further advance into the woods, with the 1st Massachusetts Regiment.

Meanwhile Tyler, discovering a favorable opening in the woods, "low down on the bottom of the stream," for a couple of howitzers in battery, sends Captain Ayres of the 5th U. S. Artillery, and a detached section (two 12-pound howitzers) of his battery, with orders to post it himself on that spot, and sends Brackett's squadron of the 2d Cavalry to his support.

No sooner does Ayres open fire on the Enemy, than he awakens a Rebel hornet's-nest. Volley after volley of musketry shows that the Bull Run bottom fairly swarms with Rebel troops, while another Rebel battery, more to the Rebel right, opens, with that already mentioned, a concentrated cross-fire upon him.

And now Richardson orders up the 12th New York, Colonel Walrath, to the left of our battery. Forming it into line-of-battle, Richardson orders it to charge through the woods upon the Enemy. Gallantly the regiment moves forward, after the skirmishers, into the woods, but, being met by a very heavy fire of musketry and artillery along the whole line of the Enemy's position, is, for the most part, thrown back in confusion—a mere fragment* remaining in line, and retreating,—while the howitzers, and Cavalry also, are withdrawn.

Meantime, however, Richardson has ordered up, and placed in line-of-battle, on the right of our battery, the 1st Massachusetts, the 2d Michigan (his own), and the 3d Michigan. The skirmishers in the woods still bravely hold their ground, undercover, and these three regiments are plucky, and anxious to assault the Enemy. Richardson proposes to lead them in a charge upon the Enemy's position, and drive him out of it; but Tyler declines to give permission, on the ground that this being "merely a reconnaissance," the object of which—ascertaining the strength and position of the Enemy—having been attained, a further attack is unnecessary. He therefore orders Richardson to "fall back in good order to our batteries on the hill,"—which he does.

Upon reaching these batteries, Richardson forms his 2d Michigan, in "close column by division," on their right, and the 1st Massachusetts and 3d Michigan, in "line of battle," on their left—the 12th New York re-forming, under cover of the woods at the rear, later on. Then, with our skirmishers thrown into the woods in front, their scattering fire, and the musketry responses of the Rebels, are drowned in the volume of sound produced by the deafening contest which ensues between our Artillery, and that of the Enemy from his batteries behind Bull Run.

This artillery-duel continues about one hour; and then seems to cease by mutual consent, about dusk—after 415 shots have been fired on the Union side, and have been responded to by an equal number from the Rebel batteries, "gun for gun"—the total loss in the engagement, on the Union side, being 83, to a total loss among the Enemy, of Thursday night, Richardson retires his brigade upon Centreville, in order to secure rations and water for his hungry and thirsty troops,—as no water has yet been found in the vicinity of the Union batteries aforesaid. On the morrow, however, when his brigade re-occupies that position, water is found in abundance, by digging for it.

This premature attack, at Blackburn's Ford, by Tyler, against orders, having failed, throws a wet blanket upon the martial spirit of McDowell's Army. In like degree is the morale of the Rebel Army increased.

It is true that Longstreet, in command of the Rebel troops at Blackburn's Ford, has not had things all his own way; that some of his artillery had to be "withdrawn;" that, as he acknowledges in his report, his brigade of three Virginia regiments (the 1st, 11th, and 17th) had "with some difficulty repelled" the Union assault upon his position; that he had to call upon General Early for re-enforcements; that Early re-enforced him with two Infantry regiments (the 7th Louisiana and 7th Virginia) at first; that one of these (the 7th Virginia) was "thrown into confusion;" that Early then brought up his own regiment (the 24th Virginia) under Lieutenant Colonel Hairston, and the entire seven guns of the "Washington Artillery;" and that but for the active "personal exertions" of Longstreet, in "encouraging the men under his command," and the great numerical superiority of the Rebels, there might have been no Union "repulse" at all. Yet still the attack has failed, and that failure, while it dispirits the Patriot Army, inspires the Rebel Army with renewed courage.

Under these circumstances, Friday, the 19th of July, is devoted to reconnaissances by the Engineer officers of the Union Army; to the cooking of the supplies, which have at last arrived; and to resting the weary and road-worn soldiers of the Union.

Let us take advantage of this halt in the advance of McDowell's "Grand Army of the United States"—as it was termed—to view the Rebel position at, and about Manassas, and to note certain other matters having an important and even determining bearing upon the issue of the impending shock-at-arms.

Beauregard has received early information of McDowell's advance from Arlington, and of his plans.

[This he admits, in his report, when he says; "Opportunely informed of the determination of the Enemy to advance on Manassas, my advanced brigades, on the night of the 16th of July, were made aware, from these headquarters, of the impending movement,"]

On Tuesday the 16th, he notifies his advanced brigades. On Wednesday, he sends a dispatch from Manassas, to Jefferson Davis, at Richmond, announcing that the Union troops have assailed his outposts in heavy force; that he has fallen back before them, on the line of Bull Run; and that he intends to make a stand at Mitchell's Ford (close to Blackburn's Ford) on that stream,—adding: if his (McDowell's) force is overwhelming, "I shall retire to the Rappahannock railroad bridge, saving my command for defense there, and future operations. Please inform Johnston of this, via Staunton, and also Holmes. Send forward any re-enforcements at the earliest possible instant, and by every possible means."

In the meantime, however, Beauregard loses no time in advantageously posting his troops. On the morning of the 18th of July, when the Union advance enters Centreville, he has withdrawn all his advanced brigades within the Rebel lines of Bull Run, resting them on the South side of that stream, from Union Mills Ford, near the Orange and Alexandria railroad bridge, up to the stone bridge over which the Warrenton Pike crosses the Run,—a distance of some six to eight miles.

Between the Rebel left, at Stone Bridge, and the Rebel right, at Union Mills Ford, are several fords across Bull Run—the general course of the stream being from the North-West to South-East, to its confluence with the Occoquan River, some twelve miles from the Potomac River.

Mitchell's Ford, the Rebel center, is about three miles to the South-West of, and about the same distance North-East from, Manassas Junction. But it may be well, right here, to locate all these fordable crossings of the rocky, precipitous, and well-wooded Bull Run stream, between the Stone Bridge and Union Mills Ford. Thus, half a mile below the Stone Bridge is Lewis's Ford; half a mile below that, Ball's Ford; half a mile below that, Island Ford; one and one-half miles below that, Mitchell's Ford—one mile below that.

Blackburn's Ford; three-quarters of a mile farther down, McLean's Ford; and nearly two miles lower down the stream, Union Mills Ford.

By Thursday morning, the 18th of July, Beauregard has advantageously posted the seven brigades into which he has organized his forces, at these various positions along his extended front, as follows:

At the Stone Bridge, Brigadier-General N. G. Evans's Seventh Brigade, of one regiment and one battalion of Infantry, two companies of Cavalry, and a battery of four six-pounders.

At Lewis's, Balls, and Island Fords—Colonel P. St. George Cocke's Fifth Brigade, of three regiments of Infantry, one battery of Artillery, and one company of Cavalry.

At Mitchell's Ford, Brigadier-General M. L. Bonham's First Brigade, of four Infantry regiments, two batteries, and six companies of Cavalry.

At Blackburn's Ford, Brigadier-General J. Longstreet's Fourth Brigade, of four Infantry regiments, with two 6-pounders.

At McLean's Ford, Brigadier-General D. R. Jones's Third Brigade of three Infantry regiments, one Cavalry company, and two 6-pounders.

At Union Mills Ford, Brigadier-General R. S. Ewell's Second Brigade, of three Infantry regiments, three Cavalry companies, and four 12-powder howitzers—Colonel Jubal A. Early's Sixth Brigade, of three Infantry regiments and three rifled pieces of Walton's Battery, being posted in the rear of, and as a support to, Ewell's Brigade.

[Johnston also found, on the 20th, the Reserve Brigade of Brig. Gen. T. H. Holmes—comprising two regiments of Infantry, Walker's Battery of Artillery, and Scott's Cavalry-with Early's Brigade, "in reserve, in rear of the right."]

The disposition and strength of Beauregard's forces at these various points along his line of defense on Bull Run stream, plainly shows his expectation of an attack on his right; but he is evidently suspicious that it may come upon his centre; for, as far back as July 8th, he had issued special orders to the effect that:

"Should the Enemy march to the attack of Mitchell's Ford, via Centreville, the following movements will be made with celerity:

"I. The Fourth Brigade will march from Blackburn's Ford to attack him on the flank and centre.

"II. The Third Brigade will be thrown to the attack of his centre and rear toward Centreville.

"III. The Second and Sixth Brigades united will also push forward and attack him in the rear by way of Centreville, protecting their own right flanks and rear from the direction of Fairfax Station and Court House.

"IV. In the event of the defeat of the Enemy, the troops at Mitchell's Ford and Stone Bridge, especially the Cavalry and Artillery, will join in the pursuit, which will be conducted with vigor but unceasing prudence, and continued until he shall have been driven beyond the Potomac."

And it is not without interest to note Beauregard's subsequent indorsement on the back of these Special Orders, that: "The plan of attack prescribed within would have been executed, with modifications affecting First and Fifth Brigades, to meet the attack upon Blackburn's Ford, but for the expected coming of General Johnston's command, which was known to be en route to join me on [Thursday] the 18th of July."

The knowledge thus possessed on Thursday, the 18th, by Beauregard, that Johnston's Army is on its way to join him, is of infinite advantage to the former. On the other hand, the complete ignorance, at this time, of McDowell on this point,—and the further fact that he has been lulled into a feeling of security on the subject, by General Scott's emphatic assurance to him that "if Johnston joins Beauregard, he shall have Patterson on his heels"—is a great disadvantage to the Union general.

Were McDowell now aware of the real Military situation, he would unquestionably make an immediate attack, with the object of crushing Beauregard before Johnston can effect a junction with him. It would then be a mere matter of detail for the armies of McDowell, McClellan, and Patterson, to bag Johnston, and bring the armed Rebellion to an inglorious and speedy end. But Providence—through the plottings of individuals within our own lines—wills it otherwise.

Long before this, Patterson has been informed by General Winfield Scott of the proposed movement by McDowell upon Manassas,—and of its date.

On Saturday, July 13th, General Scott telegraphed to Patterson: "I telegraphed to you yesterday, if not strong enough to beat the Enemy early next week, make demonstrations so as to detain him in the Valley of Winchester; but if he retreats in force toward Manassas, and it be too hazardous to follow him, then consider the route via Keys Ferry, Leesburg, etc."

On Wednesday, the 17th, Scott telegraphs to Patterson: "I have nothing official from you since Sunday (14th), but am glad to learn, through Philadelphia papers, that you have advanced. Do not let the Enemy amuse and delay you with a small force in front whilst he re-enforces the Junction with his main body. McDowell's first day's work has driven the Enemy beyond Fairfax Court House. The Junction will probably be carried by to-morrow."

On Thursday, the 18th, Patterson replies that to attack "the greatly superior force at Winchester "when the three months volunteers' time was about up, and they were threatening to leave him—would be "most hazardous" and then he asks: "Shall I attack?"

Scott answers the same day: "I have certainly been expecting you to beat the Enemy. If not, to hear that you had felt him strongly, or, at least, had occupied him by threats and demonstrations. You have been at least his equal, and, I suppose, superior in numbers. Has he not stolen a march and sent re-enforcements toward Manassas Junction? A week is enough to win victories," etc.

Patterson retorts, on the same day: "The Enemy has stolen no march upon me. I have kept him actively employed, and by threats, and reconnaissances in force, caused him to be re-enforced. I have accomplished in this respect more than the General-in-Chief asked, or could well be expected, in face of an Enemy far superior in numbers, with no line of communication to protect."

In another dispatch, to Assistant Adjutant-General Townsend (with General Scott), he says, that same afternoon of Thursday, the 18th: "I have succeeded, in accordance with the wishes of the General-in-Chief, in keeping General Johnston's Force at Winchester. A reconnaissance in force, on Tuesday, caused him to be largely re-enforced from Strasburg."

Again, on Friday, the 19th, he informs Colonel Townsend that: "The Enemy, from last information, are still at Winchester, and being re-enforced every night."

It is not until Saturday, the 20th of July, that he telegraphs to Townsend: "With a portion of his force, Johnston left Winchester, by the road to Millwood, on the afternoon of the 18th." And he adds the ridiculous statement: "His whole force was about 35,200."

Thus, despite all the anxious care of General Scott, to have Johnston's Army detained in the Shenandoah Valley, it has escaped Patterson so successfully, and entirely, that the latter does not even suspect its disappearance until the day before the pitched Battle of Bull Run is fought! Its main body has actually reached Manassas twenty-four hours before Patterson is aware that it has left Winchester!

And how is it, that Johnston gets away from Patterson so neatly? And when does he do it?

[The extraordinary conduct of General Patterson at this critical period, when everything seemed to depend upon his exertions, was afterward the subject of inquiry by the Joint-Committee on the Conduct of the War. The testimony taken by that Committee makes it clear, to any unprejudiced mind, that while Patterson himself may have been loyal to the Union, he was weak enough to be swayed from the path of duty by some of the faithless and unpatriotic officers with whom he had partly surrounded himself—and especially by Fitz John Porter, his Chief-of-staff. Let us examine the sworn testimony of two or three witnesses on this point.

General CHARLES W. SANFORD, who was second in command under Patterson, and in command of Patterson's Left Wing, testified [see pages 54-66, Report on Conduct of the War, Vol. 3, Part 2,] that he was at a Council of War held at the White House, June 29th, when the propriety of an attack on the Rebel lines at Manassas was discussed; that he objected to any such movement until Patterson was in such a position as to prevent the junction between General Johnston's Army and the troops at Manassas; that on the 6th of July, he was sent by General Scott, with four picked New York regiments, to Patterson, and (waiving his own seniority rank) reported to that General, at Williamsport; that Patterson gave him command of a division of 8,000 men (and two batteries) out of a total in his Army of 22,000; that he "delivered orders from General Scott to General Patterson, and urged a forward movement as soon as possible;" that there was "Some delay at Martinsburg, notwithstanding the urgency of our matter," but they "left there on [Monday] the 15th of July, and went in the direction of Winchester,"—down to Bunker Hill,—Patterson with two divisions going down the turnpike, and Sanford taking his division a little in advance and more easterly on the side roads so as to be in a position to flank Johnston's right; that on that afternoon (Monday, July 15) General Patterson rode up to where Sanford was locating his camp.

Continuing his testimony, General Sanford said: "I was then within about nine miles of Johnston's fortified camp at Winchester. Patterson was complimenting me upon the manner in which my regiments were located, and inquiring about my pickets, which I had informed him I had sent down about three miles to a stream below. I had driven out the Enemy's skirmishers ahead of us. They had some cavalry there. In answer to his compliments about the comfortable location I had made, I said: 'Very comfortable, General, when shall we move on?' * * * He hesitated a moment or two, and then said: 'I don't know yet when we shall move. And if I did I would not tell my own father.' I thought that was rather a queer speech to make to me under the circumstances. But I smiled and said: 'General, I am only anxious that we shall get forward, that the Enemy shall not escape us.' He replied: 'There is no danger of that. I will have a reconnaissance to-morrow, and we will arrange about moving at a very early period.' He then took his leave.

"The next day [Tuesday, July 16th], there was a reconnaissance on the Winchester turnpike, about four or five miles below the General's camp. He sent forward a section of artillery and some cavalry, and they found a post-and-log fence across the Winchester turnpike, and some of the Enemy's cavalry on the other side of it. They gave them a round of grape. The cavalry scattered off, and the reconnaissance returned. That was the only reconnaissance I heard of while we were there. My own pickets went further than that. But it was understood, the next afternoon, that we were to march forward at daylight. I sent down Col. Morell, with 40 men, to open a road down to Opequan Creek, within five miles of the camp at Winchester, on the side-roads I was upon, which would enable me, in the course of three hours, to get between Johnston and the Shenandoah River, and effectually bar his way to Manassas. I had my ammunition all distributed, and ordered my men to have 24 hours' rations in their haversacks, independent of their breakfast. We were to march at 4 o'clock the next morning. I had this road to the Opequan completed that night. I had then with me, in addition to my eight regiments amounting to about 8,000 men and a few cavalry, Doubleday's heavy United States battery of 20 and 30 pounders, and a very good Rhode Island battery. And I was willing to take the risk, whether Gen. Patterson followed me up or not, of placing myself between Johnston and the Shenandoah River, rather than let Johnston escape. And, at 4 o'clock [July 17th] I should have moved over that road for that purpose, if I had had no further orders. But, a little after 12 o'clock at night [July 16th-17th,] I received a long order of three pages from Gen. Patterson, instructing me to move on to Charlestown, which is nearly at right angles to the road I was going to move on, and twenty-two miles from Winchester. This was after I had given my orders for the other movement."

* * * * * * * * * *

'Question [by the Chairman].—And that left Johnston free? "Answer—Yes,

Sir; left him free to make his escape, which he did. * * *"

'Question.—In what direction would Johnston have had to move to get by you? "Answer—Right out to the Shenandoah River, which he forded. He found out from his cavalry, who were watching us, that we were actually leaving, and he started at 1 o'clock that same day, with 8,000 men, forded the Shenandoah where it was so deep that he ordered his men to put their cartridge-boxes on their bayonets, got out on the Leesburg road, and went down to Manassas."

"Question [by the Chairman].—Did he [Patterson] assign any reason for that movement? "Answer.—I was, of course, very indignant about it, and so were all my officers and men; so much so that when, subsequently, at Harper's Ferry, Patterson came by my camp, there was a universal groan—against all discipline, of course, and we suppressed it as soon as possible. The excuse given by Gen. Patterson was this: that he had received intelligence that he could rely upon, that Gen. Johnston had been re-enforced by 20,000 men from Manassas, and was going to make an attack upon him; and in the order which I received that night—a long order of three pages—I was ordered to occupy all the communicating roads, turning off a regiment here, and two or three regiments there, and a battery at another place, to occupy all the roads from Winchester to the neighborhood of Charlestown, and all the cross-roads, and hold them all that day, until Gen. Patterson's whole army went by me to Charlestown; and I sat seven hours in the saddle near a place called Smithfield, while Patterson, with his whole army, went by me on their way to Charlestown, he being apprehensive, as he said, of an attack from Johnston's forces."

"Question [by Mr. Odell].—You covered his movement? "Answer—Yes, Sir. Now the statement that he made, which came to me through Colonel Abercrombie, who was Patterson's brother-in-law, and commanded one division in that army, was, that Johnston had been re-enforced; and Gen. Fitz-John Porter reported the same thing to my officers. Gen. Porter was then the chief of Patterson's staff, and was a very excellent officer, and an accomplished soldier. They all had got this story, which was without the slightest shadow of foundation; for there had not a single man arrived at the camp since we had got full information that their force consisted of 20,000 men, of whom 1,800 were sick with the measles. The story was, however, that they had ascertained, by reliable information, of this re-enforcement. Where they got their information, I do not know. None such reached me; and I picked up deserters and other persons to get all the information I could; and we since have learned, as a matter of certainty, that Johnston's forces never did exceed 20,000 men there. But the excuse Patterson gave was, that Johnson had been re-enforced by 20,000 men from Manassas, and was going to attack him. That was the reason he gave then for this movement. But in this paper he has lately published, he hints at another reason—another excuse—which was that it was by order of Gen. Scott. Now, I know that the peremptory order of Gen. Scott to Gen. Patterson, repeated over and over again, was this—I was present on several occasions when telegraphic communications went from Gen. Scott to Gen. Patterson: Gen. Scott's orders to Gen. Patterson were that, if he were strong enough, he was to attack and beat Johnston. But if not, then he was to place himself in such a position as to keep Johnston employed, and prevent him from making a junction with Beauregard at Manassas. That was the repeated direction of Gen. Scott to Gen. Patterson; and it was because of Patterson's hesitancy, and his hanging back, and keeping so far beyond the reach of Johnston's camp, that I was ordered to go up there and re-enforce him, and assist him in any operations necessary to effect that object. The excuse of Gen. Patterson now is, that he had orders from Gen. Scott to move to Charlestown. Now, that is not so. But this state of things existed: Before the movement was made from Martinsburg, General Patterson suggested to General Scott that Charlestown would be a better base of operations than Martinsburg and suggested that he had better move on Charlestown, and thence make his approaches to Winchester; that it would be better to do that than to move directly to Winchester from Martinsburg; and General Scott wrote back to say that, if he found that movement a better one, he was at liberty to make it. But Gen. Patterson had already commenced his movement on Winchester direct from Martinsburg, and had got as far as Bunker Hill; so that the movement which he had formerly suggested, to Charlestown, was suppressed by his own act. But that is the pretence now given in his published speech for making the movement from Bunker Hill to Charlestown, which was a retreat, instead of the advance which the movement to Charlestown he first proposed to Gen. Scott was intended to be."

* * * * * * * * * * *

"Question [by the Chairman].—Was not that change of direction and movement to Charlestown a total abandonment of the object which you were pursuing? "Answer.—Entirely an abandonment of the main principles of the orders he was acting under."

"Question.—And of course an abandonment of the purpose for which you were there? "Answer.—Yes, Sir.

"Question [by Mr. Odell].—Was it not your understanding in leaving here, and was it not the understanding also of Gen. Scott, that your purpose in going there was to check Johnston with direct reference to the movement here? "Answer—Undoubtedly. It was in consequence of the suggestion made by me at the Council at the President's house. * * * And upon the suggestion of General Scott they wanted me to go up there and assist Patterson in this movement against Johnston, so as to carry out the point I had suggested of first checkmating Johnston before the movement against

Manassas was made here."

* * * * * * * * *

Question [by the Chairman].—Would there have been any difficulty in preventing Johnston from going to Manassas? "Answer.—None whatever."

* * * * * * * * *

"Question [by the Chairman.]—I have heard it suggested that he (Patterson) undertook to excuse this movement on the ground that the time of many of his troops had expired, and they refused to accompany him. "Answer.—That to my knowledge, is untrue. The time of none of them had expired when this movement was made. All the troops that were there were in the highest condition for the service. These three-months' men, it may be well to state to you who are not Military men, were superior to any other volunteer troops that we had, in point of discipline. They were the disciplined troops of the Country. The three-months' men were generally the organized troops of the different States—New York, Pennsylvania, etc. We had, for instance, from Patterson's own city, Philadelphia, one of the finest regiments in the service, which was turned over to me, at their own request; and the most of my regiments were disciplined and organized troops. They were all in fine condition, anxious, zealous, and earnest for a fight. They thought they were going to attack Johnston's camp at Winchester. Although I had suggested to Gen. Patterson that there was no necessity for that, the camp being admirably fortified with many of their heavy guns from Norfolk, I proposed to him to place ourselves between Johnston and the Shenandoah, which would have compelled him to fight us there, or to remain in his camp, either of which would have effected General Scott's object. If I had got into a fight, it was very easy, over this road I had just been opening, for Patterson to have re-enforced me and to have come up to the fight in time. The proposition was to place ourselves between Johnston's fortified camp and the Shenandoah, where his fortified camp would have been of no use to him."

"Question.—Even if you had received a check there, it would have prevented his junction with the forces at Manassas? "Answer.—Yes, Sir; I would have risked a battle with my own division rather than Johnston should have escaped. If he had attacked me, I could have taken a position where I could have held it, while Patterson could have fallen upon him and repulsed him."

"Question [by Mr. Odell].—Had you any such understanding with Patterson? "Answer.—I told him I would move down on this side-road in advance, leaving Gen. Patterson to sustain me if I got into a fight. So, on the other hand, if he should attack Patterson, I was near enough to fall upon Johnston's flank and to support Patterson. By using this communication of mine to pass Opequan Creek—where, I had informed Patterson, I had already pushed forward my pickets, [200 men in the day and 400 more at night,] to prevent the Enemy from burning the bridge—it would have enabled me to get between Johnston and the Shenandoah River. On the morning [Wednesday, July 17th] of our march to Charlestown, Stuart's cavalry, which figured so vigorously at Bull Run, was upon my flank all day. They were apparently about 800 strong. I saw them constantly on my flank for a number of miles. I could distinguish them, with my glass, with great ease. Finally, they came within about a mile of the line of march I was pursuing and I sent a battery around to head them off, and the 12th Regiment across the fields in double-quick time to take them in the rear. I thought I had got them hemmed in. But they broke down the fences, and went across the country to Winchester, and I saw nothing more of them. They were then about eight miles from Winchester, and must have got there in the course of a couple of hours. That day [Wednesday, the 17th] at 10 o'clock—as was ascertained from those who saw him crossing the Shenandoah—Johnston started from Winchester with 8,000 men, forded the Shenandoah, and got to Manassas on Friday night; and his second in command started the next day with all the rest of the available troops—something like 9,000 men; leaving only the sick, and a few to guard them, in the camp at Winchester—and they arrived at the battle-field in the midst of the fight, got out of the cars, rushed on the battle-field, and turned the scale. I have no doubt that, if we had intercepted Johnston, as we ought to have done, the battle of Bull Run would have been a victory for us instead of a defeat. Johnston was undoubtedly the ablest general they had in their army."

Colonel CRAIG BIDDLE, testified that he was General Patterson's aide-de-camp at the time. In answer to a question by the Chairman, he continued:

"Answer.—I was present, of course, at all the discussions. The discussion at Martinsburg was as to whether or not General Patterson should go on to Winchester. General Patterson was very full of that himself. He was determined to go to Winchester; but the opinions of all the regular officers who were with him, were against it. The opinions of all the men in whose judgment I had any confidence, were against it. They seemed to have the notion that General Patterson had got his Irish blood up by the fight we had had at Falling Waters, and was bound to go ahead. He decided upon going ahead, against the remonstrances of General [Fitz John] Porter, who advised against it. He told me he considered he had done his duty, and said no more. The movement was delayed in consequence of General Stone's command not being able to move right away. It was then evident that there was so much opposition to it that the General was induced to call a council of the general officers in his command, at which I was present. They were unanimously opposed to the advance. That was at Martinsburg."

* * * * * * * *

"Question.—While at Bunker Hill, the night before you left there, were any orders issued to march in the evening? "Answer.—I think there were such orders."

"Question.—Did not General Patterson issue orders at Bunker Hill, the night before you marched to Charlestown, for an attack on the Enemy? "Answer.—I think such orders were written. I do not think they were issued. I think General Patterson was again persuaded not to make an advance."

Colonel R. BUTLER PRICE, Senior aide to Patterson, testified as follows:

* * * * * * * * *

"Question [by Mr. Gooch].—Was it not the intention to move from Bunker Hill to Winchester? "Answer.—Yes, Sir. At one time General Patterson had given an order to move from Bunker Hill to Winchester. He was very unwilling to leave Johnston even at Winchester without attacking him; and on the afternoon before we left Bunker Hill he decided to attack him, notwithstanding his strong force."

"Question.—Behind his intrenchments? "Answer.—Yes, Sir; it went so far that his order was written by his adjutant, General [Fitz John] Porter. It was very much against the wishes of General [Fitz John] Porter; and he asked General Patterson if he would send for Colonel Abercrombie and Colonel Thomas and consult them on the movement. General Patterson replied: No, Sir; for I know they will attempt to dissuade me from it, and I have made up my mind to fight Johnston under all circumstances. That was the day before we left Bunker Hill. Then Colonel [Fitz John] Porter asked to have Colonel Abercrombie and Colonel Thomas sent for and consulted as to the best manner to carry out his wishes. He consented, and they came, and after half an hour they dissuaded him from it."

"Question.—At that time General Patterson felt it was so important to attack Johnston that he had determined to do it? "Answer.—Yes, Sir; the order was not published, but it was written."

"Question.—You understood General Patterson to be influenced to make that attempt because he felt there was a necessity for detaining Johnston? "Answer.—Yes, Sir; to detain him as long as he possibly could."

"Question.—That order was not countermanded until late on Tuesday, the 16th, was it? "Answer.—That order never was published. It was written; but, at the earnest solicitation of Colonel [Fitz John] Porter, it was withheld until he could have a consultation with Colonel Abercrombie and Colonel Thomas."]

It is about 1 o'clock on the morning of Thursday, July 18th,—that same day which witnesses the preliminary Battle of Blackburn's Ford—that Johnston, being at Winchester, and knowing of Patterson's peculiarly inoffensive and timid movement to his own left and rear, on Charlestown, receives from the Rebel Government at Richmond, a telegraphic dispatch, of July 17th, in these words: "General Beauregard is attacked. To strike the Enemy a decisive blow, a junction of all your effective force will be needed. If practicable, make the movement. * * * In all the arrangements exercise your discretion."

Johnston loses no time in deciding that it is his duty to prevent, if possible, disaster to Beauregard's Army; that to do this he must effect a junction with him; and that this necessitates either an immediate fight with, and defeat of, Patterson,—which may occasion a fatal delay—or else, that Union general must be eluded. Johnston determines on the latter course.

Leaving his sick, with some militia to make a pretense of defending the town in case of attack, Johnston secretly and rapidly marches his Army, of 9,000 effective men, Southeasterly from Winchester, at noon of Thursday, the 18th; across by a short cut, wading the Shenandoah River, and then on through Asby's Gap, in the Blue Ridge, that same night; still on, in the same direction, to a station on the Manassas Gap railroad, known as Piedmont, which is reached by the next (Friday) morning,—the erratic movements of Stuart's Cavalry entirely concealing the manoeuvre from the knowledge of Patterson.

From Piedmont, the Artillery and Cavalry proceed to march the remaining twenty-five miles, or so, to Manassas Junction, by the roads. The 7th and 8th Georgia Regiments of Bartow's Brigade, with Jackson's Brigade,—comprising the 2d, 4th, 5th, 27th and 33d Virginia Regiments—are embarked on the cars, and hurriedly sent in advance, by rail, to Manassas, reaching there on that same (Friday) afternoon and evening. These are followed by General Johnston, with Bee's Brigade—comprising the 4th Alabama, 2d Mississippi, and a battalion of the 11th Mississippi—which arrive at Manassas about noon of Saturday, the 20th of July, the balance of Johnston's Infantry being billed for arrival that same day, or night.

Upon Johnston's own arrival at Manassas, Saturday noon,—the very day that Patterson ascertains that "the bird has flown,"—after assuming command, by virtue of seniority, he proceeds to examine Beauregard's position. This he finds "too extensive, and the ground too densely wooded and intricate," to be learned quickly, and hence he is impelled to rely largely upon Beauregard for information touching the strength and positions of both the Rebel and Union Armies.

Beauregard has now 21,833 men, and 29 pieces of artillery of his own "Army of the Potomac." Johnston's and Holmes's junction with him has raised the Rebel total to 32,000 effectives, and 55 guns. McDowell, on the other hand, who started with 30,000 effectives, finds himself on the 19th—owing to the departure of one of his regiments and a battery of Artillery, because of the expiration of their term of enlistment,—with but "28,000 men at the utmost."—[Comte de Paris.]

On the evening of Saturday, the 20th of July, Johnston and Beauregard hold an important consultation. The former feels certain that Patterson, with his more than 20,000 effectives, will now lose no time in essaying a junction with McDowell's Army, and that such junction will probably be effected by July 22nd. Hence he perceives the necessity of attacking McDowell, and if possible, with the combined Rebel Forces, whipping him before Patterson can come up to his assistance.

At this consultation it is agreed by the two Rebel generals to assume the offensive, at once. Beauregard proposes a plan of battle—which is an immediate general advance of the Rebel centre and left, concentrating, from all the fords of Bull Run, upon Centreville, while the Rebel right advances toward Sangster's cross-roads, ready to fall either on Centreville, or upon Fairfax Court House, in its rear, according to circumstances.

The plan proposed, is accepted at once by Johnston. The necessary order is drawn up by Beauregard that night; and at half past four o'clock on Sunday morning, July 21st, Johnston signs the written order. Nothing now remains, apparently, but the delivery of the order to the Rebel brigade commanders, a hurried preparation for the forward movement, and then the grand attack upon McDowell, at Centreville.

Already, no doubt, the fevered brain of Beauregard pictures, in his vivid imagination, the invincible thunders of his Artillery, the impetuous advance of his Infantry, the glorious onset of his Cavalry, the flight and rout of the Union forces, his triumphal entry into Washington—Lincoln and Scott and the Congress crouching at his feet—and the victorious South and conquered North acclaiming him Dictator! The plan is Beauregard's own, and Beauregard is to have command. Hence all the glory of capturing the National Capital, must be Beauregard's. Why not? But "man proposes, and God disposes." The advance and attack, are, in that shape, never to be made.

McDowell, in the meantime, all unconscious of what has transpired in the Shenandoah Valley, and between there and Manassas; never dreaming for an instant that Patterson has failed to keep Johnson there—even if he has not attacked and defeated him; utterly unsuspicious that his own lessened Union Army has now to deal with the Forces of Johnston and Beauregard combined—with a superior instead of an inferior force; is executing a plan of battle which he has decided upon, and announced to his general officers, on that same Saturday evening, at his Headquarters in Centreville.

Instead of attempting to turn the Enemy's right, and cut off his communications with Richmond and the South, McDowell has now determined to attack the Enemy's left, cut his communication, via the Manassas Gap railroad, with Johnston's Army,—still supposed by him to be in the Valley of the Shenandoah—and, taking him in the left flank and rear, roll him upon Manassas, in disorder and defeat—with whatever might follow.

That is the plan—in its general features. In executing it, Blenker's Brigade of Miles's Division is to remain at Centreville as a reserve, throwing up intrenchments about its Heights, upon which to fall back, in case of necessity; Davies's Brigade of the same Division, with Richardson's Brigade of Tyler's Division—as the Left Wing—are to demonstrate at Blackburn's Ford, toward the Enemy's right; Tyler's other three brigades, under Keyes, Schenck, and Sherman, are to feign an attack on the Enemy's left, posted behind the strongly-defended Stone Bridge over which the Warrenton turnpike, running Westward, on its way from Centreville to Warrenton, crosses Bull Run stream; while the strong divisions under Hunter and Heintzelman—forming McDowell's Right Wing—are to follow Tyler's Division Westward down the turnpike to a point within one mile and a half of the Stone Bridge, thence, by cross-road, diverge several miles to the North, then sweep around gradually to the West, and then Southwardly over Bull Run at Sudley Springs Ford, swooping down the Sudley road upon the Enemy's left flank and rear, near Stone Bridge, rolling it back toward his center, while Tyler's remaining three brigades cross the bridge and join in the assault. That is the whole plan in a nutshell.

It has been McDowell's intention to push forward, from Centreville along the Warrenton Pike a few miles, on the evening of this Military conference; but he makes his first mistake, in allowing himself to be dissuaded from that, by those, who, in his own words, "have the greatest distance to go," and who prefer "starting early in the morning and making but one move."
The attacking divisions now have orders to march at 2:30 A. M., in order "to avoid the heat," which is excessive. Tyler's three immediate brigades—or some of them—are slow in starting Westward, along the Warrenton Pike, to the Stone Bridge; and this leads to a two or three hours delay of the divisions of Hunter and Heintzelman, before they can follow that Pike beyond Centreville, and commence the secret detour to their right, along the cross-road leading to Sudley Springs.
At 6:30 A.M., Tyler's Artillery gets into position, to cannonade the Enemy's batteries, on the West Bank of Bull Run, commanding the Stone Bridge, and opens fire. Half an hour before this, (at 6 A.M.), the Rebel artillerists, posted on a hill South of the Pike, and 600 yards West of the bridge, have caught sight of Tyler's Union blue-jackets. Those of the Rebel gunners whose eyes are directed to the North-East, soon see, nearly a mile away, up the gradual slope, a puff of blue smoke. Immediately the bang of a solitary rifle cannon is heard, and the scream of a rifled shot as it passes over their heads. At intervals, until past 9 A.M., that piece and others in the same position, keep hammering away at the Rebel left, under Evans, at Stone Bridge.
The Rebel response to this cannonade, is very feeble. McDowell observes

this. He suspects there has been a weakening of the Enemy's force at the bridge, in order to strengthen his right for some purpose. And what can that purpose be, but to throw his augmented right upon our left, at Blackburn's Ford, and so, along the ridge-road, upon Centreville? Thus McDowell guesses, and guesses well. To be in readiness to protect his own left and rear, by reenforcing Miles's Division, at Centreville and along the ridge to Blackburn's Ford, he temporarily holds back Howard's Brigade of Heintzelman's Division at the point where the cross-road to Sudley Springs Ford—along which Hunter's Division, followed by the Brigades of Franklin and Wilcox, of Heintzelman's Division, have already gone—intersects the Warrenton Pike.

It is 9 o'clock. Beauregard, as yet unaware of McDowell's new plan, sends an order to Ewell, on his right, to hold himself ready "to take the offensive, at a moment's notice,"—and directing that Ewell be supported in his advance, toward Sangster's cross-roads and the rear of Centreville, by Holmes's Brigade. In accordance with that order, Ewell, who is "at Union Mills and its neighborhood," gets his brigade ready, and Holmes moves up to his support. After waiting two hours, Ewell receives another order, for both Ewell and Holmes "to resume their places." Something must have occurred since 9 o'clock, to defeat Beauregard's plan of attack on Centreville—with all its glorious consequences! What can it be? We shall see.

While Tyler's Artillery has been cannonading the Rebel left, under Evans, at Stone Bridge,—fully impressed with the prevailing Union belief that the bridge is not only protected by strong masked batteries, heavy supports of Infantry, and by abatis as well as other defenses, but is also mined and ready to be blown up at the approach of our troops, when in reality the bridge is not mined, and the Rebel force in men and guns at that point has been greatly weakened in anticipation of Beauregard's projected advance upon Centreville,—the Union column, under Hunter and Heintzelman, is advancing from Centreville, in the scorching heat and suffocating dust of this tropical July morning, slowly, but surely, along the Warrenton Pike and the cross-road to Sudley Springs Ford—a distance of some eight miles of weary and toilsome marching for raw troops in such a temperature—in this order: Burnside's Brigade, followed by Andrew Porter's Brigade,—both of Hunter's Division; then Franklin's Brigade, followed by Willcox's Brigade,—both of Heintzelman's Division.

It is half past 9 o'clock; before Burnside's Brigade has crossed the Bull Run stream, at Sudley's Ford, and the head of Andrew Porter's Brigade commences to ford it. The troops are somewhat slow in crossing. They are warm, tired, thirsty, and as to dust,—their hair and eyes and nostrils and mouths are full of it, while most of the uniforms, once blue, have become a dirty gray. The sky is clear. The sun already is fiercely hot. The men stop to drink and fill their canteens. It is well they do.

McDowell, who has been waiting two or three hours at the turn, impatient at the delay, has ridden over to the front of the Flanking column, and now reaches Sudley's Ford. He feels that much valuable time is already lost. His plan has, in a measure, been frustrated by delay. He had calculated on crossing Bull Run, at Sudley's Ford, and getting to the rear of the Enemy's position, at Stone Bridge, before a sufficient Rebel force could be assembled to contest the Union advance. He sends back an aide with orders to the regimental commanders in the rear, to "break from column, and hurry forward separately, as fast as possible." Another aide he sends, with orders to Howard to bring his brigade across-fields. To Tyler he also sends orders to "press forward his attack, as large bodies of the Enemy are passing in front of him to attack the division (Hunter's) which has passed over."

It may here be explained, that the Sudley road, running about six miles South-Southeasterly from Sudley Springs Ford to Manassas Junction, is crossed at right angles, about two miles South of the Springs, by the Warrenton Pike, at a point about one mile and a half West of the Stone Bridge. For nearly a mile South of Sudley Ford, the Sudley road passes through thick woods on the left, and alternate patches of wooded and cleared lands on the right. The country farther South, opens into rolling fields, occasionally cut by transverse gullies, and patched with woods. This is what Burnside's Brigade beholds, as it marches Southward, along the Sudley road, this eventful morning.

Thus far, the cannonade of Tyler's batteries, and the weak return-fire of the Rebel Artillery, at Stone Bridge, over two miles South-East of Sudley Ford, is about the only music by which the Union march has kept time.

But now, as Burnside's foremost regiment emerges from the woods, at half past 10 o'clock, the Artillery of the Enemy opens upon it.

Let us see how this happens. Evans's Brigade, defending the Stone Bridge, and constituting the Enemy's extreme left, comprises, as has already been mentioned, Sloan's 4th South Carolina Regiment, Wheat's Louisiana battalion, Terry's squadron of Virginia Cavalry, and Davidson's section of Latham's Battery of six-pounders.

Earlier in the morning Evans has supposed, from the cannonade of Tyler's batteries among the pines on the hills obliquely opposite the Enemy's left, as well as from the sound of the cannonade of the Union batteries away down the stream on the Enemy's right, near Blackburn's Ford, that McDowell is about to make an attack upon the whole front of the Rebel line of defense along Bull Run—by way of the Stone Bridge, and the various fords below it, which cross that stream. But by 10 o'clock, that Rebel general begins to feel doubtful, suspicious, and uneasy. Despite the booming of Tyler's guns, he has caught in the distance the rumbling sounds of Hunter's Artillery wheels.

Evans finds himself pondering the meaning of those long lines of dust, away to his left; and then, like a flash, it bursts upon him, that all this Military hubbub in his front, and far away to his right, is but a feint; that the real danger is somehow connected with that mysterious far-away rumble, and those lines of yellow dust; that the main attack is to be on the unprepared left and rear of the Rebel position!

No sooner has the Rebel brigade-commander thus divined the Union plan of attack, than he prepares, with the limited force at his command, to thwart it. Burnside and he are about equidistant, by this time, from the intersection of the Sudley road, running South, with the Warrenton Pike, running West. Much depends upon which of them shall be the first to reach it,—and the instinctive, intuitive knowledge of this, spurs Evans to his utmost energy. He leaves four of his fifteen companies, and Rogers's section of the Loudoun Artillery,—which has come up from Cocke's Brigade, at the ford below—to defend the approaches to the Stone Bridge, from the East side of Bull Run,—and, with the other eleven companies, and Latham's half-battery, he hurries Westward, along the Warrenton Pike, toward the Sudley road-crossing, to resist the impending Union attack.

It is now 10:30 o'clock, and, as he hurries along, with anxious eyes, scanning the woods at the North, he suddenly catches the glitter of Burnside's bayonets coming down through them, East of the Sudley road, in "column of regiments" toward Young's Branch—a small stream turning, in a Northern and Southern loop, respectively above and below the Warrenton Pike, much as the S of a prostrate dollar-mark twines above and below its horizontal line, the vicinity of which is destined to be hotly-contested ground ere night-fall.

[Says Captain D. P. Woodbury, U. S. corps of engineers, and who, with Captain Wright, guided the divisions of Hunter and Heintzelman in making the detour to the upper part of Bull Run: "At Sudley's Mills we lingered about an hour to give the men and horses water and a little rest before going into action, our advance guard in the mean time going ahead about three quarters of a mile. Resuming our march, we emerged from the woods about one mile South of the ford, and came upon a beautiful open valley about one and a quarter miles square, bounded on the right or West by a wooded ridge, on the Fast by the rough spurs or bluffs of Bull Run, on the North by an open plain and ridge, on which our troops began to form, and on the South by another ridge, on which the Enemy was strongly posted, with woods behind their backs. The Enemy was also in possession of the bluffs of Bull Run on our left."]

Sending word to Headquarters, Evans pushes forward and gaining Buck Ridge, to the North of the Northern loop of Young's Branch, forms his line-of-battle upon that elevation—which somewhat compensates him for the inferiority of his numbers—nearly at right angles to the Bull Run line; rapidly puts his Artillery in position; the Rebel guns open on Burnside's advance—their hoarse roar soon supplemented by the rattle of Rebel musketry, and the answering roar and rattle of the Union onset; and the Battle of Bull Run has commenced!

It is after 10:30 A.M., and Beauregard and Johnston are upon an eminence in the rear of the centre of the Enemy's Bull Run line. They have been there since 8 o'clock. An hour ago, or more, their Signal Officer has reported a large body of Union troops crossing the Bull Run Valley, some two or three miles above the Stone Bridge; upon the strength of which, Johnston has ordered Bee's Brigade from near Cocke's position, with Hampton's Legion and Stonewall Jackson's Brigade from near Bonham's left, to move to the Rebel left, at Stone Bridge; and these troops are now hastening thither, guided by the sound of the guns.

The artillery-firing is also heard by Johnston and Beauregard, but intervening wooded slopes prevent them from determining precisely whence it comes. Beauregard, with a badly-organized staff, is chaffing over the delay that has occurred in carrying out his own plan of battle. He is waiting to hear of the progress of the attack which he has ordered upon the Union Army,—supposed by him to be at Centreville,—and especially as to the advance of his right toward Sangster's Station. In the meantime also,— from early morning,—the Rebel commanders have heard heavy firing in the direction of Blackburn's Ford, toward their right, where the Artillery attached to the brigades of Davies and Richardson, constituting McDowell's Left Wing, is demonstrating in a lively manner, in accordance with McDowell's plan.

It is 11 o'clock. Beauregard has become satisfied that his orders for the Rebel advance and attack on Centreville, have failed or miscarried. His plan is abandoned, and the orders countermanded. At the same time the growing volume of artillery-detonations upon the left of the Bull Run line of defense—together with the clouds of dust which indicate the route of march of Hunter's and Heintzelman's Divisions from near Centreville to the point of conflict, satisfies both Johnston and Beauregard, that a serious attack is imperilling the Rebel left.

Beauregard at once proposes to Johnston "a modification of the abandoned plan," viz.: "to attack with the" Rebel "right, while the left stands on the defensive." But rapidly transpiring events conspire to make even the modified plan impracticable.

Johnston, convinced by the still growing volume of battle-sounds on the Rebel left, that the main attack of McDowell is being made there, urges Beauregard to strengthen the left, as much as possible; and, after that general has sent orders to this end,—to Holmes and Early to come up with their Brigades from Union Mills Ford, moving "with all speed to the sound of the firing," and to Bonham to promptly send up, from Mitchell's Ford, a battery and two of his regiments—both he and Beauregard put spurs to their horses, and gallop at full speed toward the firing, four miles away on their left,—stopping on the way only long enough for Johnston to order his Chief-of-artillery, Colonel Pendleton, to "follow, with his own, and Alburtis's Batteries."

Meanwhile let us return and witness the progress of the battle, on the Rebel left,—where we were looking on, at 10:30 o'clock. Evans had then just posted his eleven companies of Infantry on Buck Ridge, with one of his two guns on his left, near the Sudley road, and the other not far from the Robinson House, upon the Northern spur of the elevated plateau just South of Young's Branch, and nearly midway between the Sudley road and Stone Bridge.

The battle, as we have seen, has opened. As Burnside's Brigade appears on the slope, to the North of Buck Ridge (or Hill), it is received by a rapid, well-sustained, and uncomfortable, but not very destructive fire, from Evans's Artillery, and, as the Union regiments press forward, in column, full of impulsive ardor, the Enemy welcomes the head of the column with a hot musketry-fire also, delivered from the crest of the elevation behind which the Rebel Infantry lie flat upon the ground.

This defense by Evan's demi-Brigade still continues, although half an hour, or more, has elapsed. Burnside has not yet been able to dislodge the Enemy from the position. Emboldened to temerity by this fact, Major Wheat's Louisiana battalion advances through the woods in front, upon Burnside, but is hurled back by a galling fire, which throws it into disorder and flight.

At this moment, however, the brigades of Bee and Bartow—comprising the 7th and 8th Georgia, 2nd Mississippi, 4th Alabama, 6th North Carolina, and two companies of the 11th Mississippi, with Imboden's Battery of four pieces—recently arrived with Johnston from Winchester, come up, form on the right of Sloan's 4th South Carolina Regiment, while Wheat rallies his remnant on Sloan's left, now resting on the Sudley road, and the whole new Rebel line opens a hot fire upon Burnside's Brigade.

Hunter, for the purpose of better directing the Union attack, is at this moment rapidly riding to the left of the Union line,—which is advancing Southwardly, at right angles to Bull Run stream and the old line of Rebel defense thereon. He is struck by the fragment of a shell, and carried to the rear.

Colonel John S. Slocum's, 2nd Rhode Island, Regiment, with Reynold's Rhode Island Battery (six 13-pounders), having been sent to the front of Burnside's left, and being closely pressed by the Enemy, Burnside's own regiment the 1st Rhode Island, is gallantly led by Major Balch to the support of the 2nd, and together they handsomely repulse the Rebel onset. Burnside now sends forward Martin's 71st New York, with its two howitzers, and Marston's 2nd New Hampshire,—his whole Brigade, of four regiments and a light artillery battery, being engaged with the heavy masked battery (Imboden's and two other pieces), and nearly seven full regiments of the Enemy.

The regiments of Burnside's Brigade are getting considerably cut up. Colonels Slocum and Marston, and Major Balch, are wounded. There is some confusion in the ranks, and the Rhode Island Battery is in danger of capture, when General Andrew Porter—whose own brigade has just reached the field and is deploying to the right of Burnside's—succeeds Hunter in command of the division, and rides over to his left. Burnside asks him for Sykes's battalion of regulars, which is accordingly detached from the extreme right of Andrew Porter's Division, rapidly forms on the left, in support of the Rhode Island Battery, and opens a hot and effective fire which, in connection with the renewed fire of Burnside's rallied regiments, and the opening artillery practice of Griffin's Battery—that has just come up at a gallop and gone into a good position upon an eminence to the right of Porter's Division, and to the right of the Sudley road looking South— fairly staggers the Enemy.

And now the brigades of Sherman and Keyes, having been ordered across Bull Run by General Tyler, are seen advancing from Poplar Ford, at the rear of our left,—Sherman's Brigade, headed by Corcoran's 69th New York Regiment, coming up on Burnside's left, while Keyes's Brigade is following, to the left again of, Sherman.

[Sherman, in his Official Report, after mentioning the receipt by him of Tyler's order to "cross over with the whole brigade to the assistance of Colonel Hunter"—which he did, so far as the Infantry was concerned, but left his battery under Ayres behind, on account of the impassability of the bluff on the Western bank of Bull Run—says: "Early in the day, when reconnoitering the ground, I had seen a horseman descend from a bluff in our front, cross the stream, and show himself in the open field, and, inferring we could cross over at the same point, I sent forward a company as skirmishers, and followed with the whole brigade, the New York Sixty-ninth leading."

This is evidently the ford at the elbow of Bull Run, to the right of Sherman's front, which is laid down on the Army-maps as "Poplar Ford," and which McDowell's engineers had previously discovered and mapped; and to which Major Barnard of the U. S. Engineer Corps alludes when, in his Official Report, he says: "Midway between the Stone Bridge and Sudley Spring our maps indicated another ford, which was said to be good."

The Comte de Paris, at page 241, vol. I. of his admirable "History of the Civil War in America," and perhaps other Military historians, having assumed and stated—upon the strength of this passage in Sherman's Report—that "the Military instinct" of that successful soldier had "discovered" this ford; and the impression being thus conveyed, however undesignedly, to their readers, that McDowell's Engineer corps, after spending two or three days in reconnaissances, had failed to find the ford which Sherman had in a few minutes "discovered" by "Military instinct;" it is surely due to the truth of Military history, that the Engineers be fairly credited with the discovery and mapping of that ford, the existence of which should also have been known to McDowell's brigade commanders.

If, on the other hand, the Report of the Rebel Captain Arthur L. Rogers, of the Loudoun Artillery, to General Philip St. George Cocke, be correct, it would seem that Sherman attempted to cross Bull Run lower down than Poplar Ford, which is "about one mile above the Stone Bridge," but was driven back by the fire of Rogers's guns to cross at that particular ford; for Rogers, in that Report, says that about 11 o'clock A. M., the first section of the Loudoun Artillery, under his command, "proceeded to the crest of the hill on the West Side of Bull Run, commanding Stone Bridge. * * * Here." continues he, "I posted my section of Artillery, and opened a brisk fire upon a column of the Enemy's Infantry, supposed to be two regiments, advancing towards me, and supported by his battery of rifled cannon on the hills opposite. These poured into my section a steady fire of shot and shell. After giving them some fifty rounds, I succeeded in heading his column, and turned it up Bull Run to a ford about one mile above Stone Bridge, where, with the regiments which followed, they crossed, and proceeded to join the rest of the Enemy's forces in front of the main body of our Army."]

Before this developing, expanding, and advancing attack of the Union forces, the Rebel General Bee, who—since his coming up to support Evans, with his own and Bartow's Brigades, to which had since been added Hampton's Legion,—has been in command of this new Rebel line of defense upon the left of the Bull Run line, concludes that that attack is getting too strong for him, and orders his forces to retreat to the Southward, and re-form on a second line, parallel to their present line, and behind the rising ground at their rear. They do so, somewhat faster than he desires. The whole line of the Rebel centre gives way, followed by the wings, as far as the victorious Union troops can see.

We must be blind if we cannot perceive that thus far, the outlook, from the Union point of view,—despite numberless mistakes of detail, and some, perhaps, more general in their character—is very good. The "Boys in Blue" are irresistibly advancing, driving the "Rebel Gray" back and back, without let or hindrance, over the Buck Hill ridge, over Young's Branch, back to, and even over, the Warrenton Pike. Time, to be sure, is flying—valuable time; but the Enemy also is retiring.—There is some slight confusion in parts of our own ranks; but there is much more in his. At present, we have decidedly the best of it. McDowell's plan has been, thus far, successful. Will that success continue? We shall see.

Heintzelman's Division is coming, up from the rear, to the Union right—Franklin's Brigade, made up of the 5th and 11th Massachusetts, and 1st Minnesota, with Ricketts's splendid battery of six 10-pounder Parrotts, forming on the right of Andrew Porter's Brigade and Division; while Willcox's demi-Brigade, with its 11th ("Fire Zouaves") and 38th New York—having left Arnold's Battery of four pieces, with the 1st Michigan as its support, posted on a hill commanding Sudley's Ford—comes in, on the right of Franklin, thus forming the extreme right of the advancing Union line of attack.

As our re-enforcing brigades come up, on our right, and on our left, the Enemy falls back, more and more discouraged and dismayed. It seems to him, as it does to us, "as though nothing can stop us." Jackson, however, is now hurrying up to the relief of the flying and disordered remnants of Bee's, Bartow's, and Evans's Brigades; and these subsequently rally, with Hampton's Legion, upon Jackson's strong brigade of fresh troops, so that, on a third new line, to which they have been driven back, they soon have—6,500 Infantry, 13 pieces of Artillery, and Stuart's cavalry—posted in a belt of pines which fringes the Southern skirt of the Henry House plateau—in a line-of-battle which, with its left resting upon the Sudley road, three-quarters of a mile South of its intersection with the Warrenton Pike, is the irregular hypothenuse of a right-angled triangle, formed by itself and those two intersecting roads, to the South-East of such intersection. It is within this right-angled triangular space that the battle, now proceeding, bids fair to rage most fiercely.

Johnston and Beauregard, riding up from their rear, reach this new (third) line to which the Rebel troops have been driven, about noon. They find the brigades of Bee, Bartow, and Evans, falling back in great disorder, and taking shelter in a wooded ravine, South of the Robinson House and of the Warrenton Pike. Hampton's Legion, which has just been driven backward over the Pike, with great loss, still holds the Robinson House. Jackson, however, has reached the front of this line of defense, with his brigade of the 2nd, 4th, 5th, 27th, and 33rd Virginia Infantry, and Pendleton's Battery—all of which have been well rested, since their arrival, with other brigades of Johnston's Army of the Shenandoah, from Winchester, a day or two back.

As Jackson comes up, on the left of "the ravine and woods occupied by the mingled remnants of Bee's, Bartow's and Evans's commands," he posts Imboden's, Stanard's, and Pendleton's Batteries in line, "below the brim of the Henry House plateau," perhaps one-eighth of a mile to the East-Southeastward of the Henry House, at his centre; Preston's 4th Virginia, and Echol's 27th Virginia, at the rear of the battery-line; Harper's 5th Virginia, with Radford's Cavalry, at its right; and, on its left, Allen's 2nd Virginia; with Cumming's 33rd Virginia to the left of that again, and Stuart's

Cavalry covering the Rebel left flank.

It is about this time that the chief Rebel generals find their position so desperate, as to necessitate extraordinary measures, and personal exposure, on their part. Now it is, that Jackson earns the famous sobriquet which sticks to him until he dies.

[Bee approaches Jackson—so goes the story, according to Swinton; he points to the disordered remnants of his own brigade mingled with those of the brigades of Bartow and Evans huddled together in the woods, and exclaims: "General, they are beating us back!" "Sir," responds Jackson, drawing himself up, severely, "We'll give them the bayonet!" And Bee, rushing back among his confused troops, rallies them with the cry: "There is Jackson, standing like a Stone wall! Let us determine to die here, and we will conquer."]

Now it is, that Johnston and Beauregard, accompanied by their staffs, ride backward and forward among the Rebel ranks, rallying and encouraging them. Now it is, that, Bee and Bartow and Hampton being wounded, and the Lieutenant-Colonel of the Hampton Legion killed, Beauregard leads a gallant charge of that legion in person. And now it is, that Johnston himself, finding all the field-officers of the 4th Alabama disabled, "impressively and gallantly charges to the front" with the colors of that regiment at his side!

These conspicuous examples of bravery, inspire the Rebel troops with fresh courage, at this admittedly "critical" moment.

Johnston now assigns to Beauregard the chief "command of the left" of the Bull Run line,—that is to say, the chief command of the Enemy's new line of defense, which, as we have seen, is on the left of, and at right angles to, the old Bull Run line—while he himself, riding back to the Lewis House, resumes "the command of the whole field."

On his way to his rear, Johnston orders Cocke to send reenforcements to Beauregard. He also dispatches orders to hurry up to that Rebel general's support, the brigades of Holmes and Early from near the Union Mills Ford, and that of Bonham from Mitchell's Ford,—Ewell with his brigade, being also directed to "follow with all speed" from Union Mills Ford-making a total of over 10,000 fresh troops.

From the "commanding elevation" of the Lewis House, Johnston can observe the position of the Union forces beyond Bull Run, at Blackburn's Ford and Stone Bridge; the coming of his own re-enforcing brigades from far down the valley, toward Manassas; and the manoeuvres of our advancing columns under McDowell.

As the battle proceeds, the Enemy's strength on the third new line of defense increases, until he has 22 guns, 260 Cavalry, and 12 regiments of Infantry, now engaged. It is interesting to observe also, that, of these, 16 of the guns, 9 of the regiments, and all of the Cavalry (Stuart's), belong to Johnston's Army of the Shenandoah, while only 6 guns and 3 Infantry regiments thus engaged, belong to Beauregard's Army of the Potomac. Thus the burden of the battle has been, and is being, borne by Johnston's, and not Beauregard's troops—in the proportion of about three of the former, to one of the latter,—which, for over two hours, maintain their position despite many successive assaults we make upon them.

It is after 2 o'clock P.M., when Howard's Brigade, of Heintzelman's Division, reaches the battle-field, almost broken down with exhaustion. By order of Heintzelman it has moved at double-quick for a mile of the way, until, under the broiling heat, it can do so no longer. The last two miles of the weary tramp, while the head of the brigade has moved at quick time, the rear, having lost distances, moves, much of the time, at a double-quick. As a consequence, many of Howard's men drop out, and absolutely faint from exhaustion.

As Howard's Brigade approaches the field, besides the ambulances and litters, conveying to the rear the wounded and dying, crowds of retreating stragglers meet and tell it to hurry along; that the Enemy has been driven back a mile; but, as it marches along, its regiments do not feel particularly encouraged by the disorganization so prevalent; and the fact that as they come into action, the thunders of the Rebel Artillery do not seem to meet an adequately voluminous response—from the Union side, seems to them, a portent of evil. Weary and fagged out, they are permitted to rest, for a while, under cover.

Up to this time, our line, increased, as it has been, by the brigades of Sherman and Keyes, on the left of Burnside, and of Franklin and Wilcox, on the right of Porter, has continued to advance victoriously. Our troops are, to be sure, considerably scattered, having been "moved from point to point" a good deal. On our left, the Enemy has been driven back nearly a mile, and Keyes's Brigade is pushing down Bull Run, under shelter of the bluffs, trying to turn the right of the Enemy's new line, and give Schenck's Brigade a better chance for crossing the Stone Bridge, still commanded by some of the Rebel guns.

Having "nothing to do" there, "several of the Union regiments" are coming over, from our left toward our right, with a view of overlapping, and turning, the Enemy's left.

It is about half past 2 o'clock. The batteries of Griffin and Ricketts have already been advanced as far as the eminence, upon our right, upon which stands the Dogan House. Supported by Lyons's gallant 14th New York Chasseurs, Griffin's and Ricketts's Batteries are still pouring a terribly destructive fire into the batteries and columns of the Enemy, now behind the brow of the Henry House hill, wherever exposed, while Palmer's seven companies of Union Cavalry are feeling the Enemy's left flank, which McDowell proposes to turn. The flags of eight Union regiments, though "borne somewhat wearily" now point toward the hilly Henry House plateau, beyond which "disordered masses of Rebels" have been seen "hastily retiring."

There is a lull in the battle. The terrible heat is exhausting to the combatants on both sides. Griffin and Ricketts have wrought such havoc with their guns, that "nothing remains to be fired at." Victory seems most surely to be ours.

Away down at his headquarters at the Lewis House, the Rebel General Johnston stands watching the progress of the battle, as it goes against him. Nervously he glances, every now and then, over his left shoulder, as if expecting something. An officer is galloping toward him, from Manassas. He comes from the office of Beauregard's Adjutant-General, at that point. He rides up and salutes. "General," says he, breathlessly, "a United States Army has reached the line of the Manassas Gap railroad, and is now but three or four miles from our left flank!"

Johnston clenches his teeth nervously. Thick beads of perspiration start from his forehead. He believes it is Patterson's Army that has followed "upon his heels" from before Winchester, faster than has been anticipated; and, as he thinks of Kirby Smith, who should long since have arrived with Elzey's Brigade—all, of his own "Army of the Shenandoah," that has not yet followed him to Manassas,—the exclamation involuntarily bursts from his lips: "Oh, for four regiments!"

[Says a correspondent and eye-witness of the battle, writing to the Richmond Dispatch, from the battle-field, July 23d: "Between two and three o'clock large numbers of men were leaving the field, some of them wounded, others exhausted by the long struggle, who gave us gloomy reports; but, as the firing on both sides continued steadily, we felt sure that our brave Southerners had not been conquered by the overwhelming hordes of the North. It is, however, due to truth to say that the result at this hour hung trembling in the balance. We had lost numbers of our most distinguished officers. Gens. Barlow and Bee had been stricken down; Lieut; Col. Johnson of the Hampton Legion had been killed; Col. Hampton had been wounded. But there was at hand a fearless general whose reputation was staked on this battle: Gen. Beauregard promptly offered to lead the Hampton Legion into action, which he executed in a style unsurpassed and unsurpassable. Gen. Beauregard rode up and down our lines, between the Enemy and his own men, regardless of the heavy fire, cheering and encouraging our troops. About this time, a shell struck his horse, taking its head off, and killing the horses of his aides, Messrs. Ferguson and Hayward. * * * Gen. Johnston also threw himself into the thickest of the fight, seizing the colors of a Georgia (Alabama) regiment, and rallying then to the charge. * * * Your correspondent heard Gen. Johnston exclaim to Gen. Cocke, just at the critical moment, 'Oh, for four regiments!' His wish was answered; for in the distance our re-enforcements appeared. The tide of battle was turned in our favor by the arrival of Gen. Kirby Smith, from Winchester, with 4,000 men of Gen. Johnston's Division. Gen. Smith heard, while on the Manassas Railroad cars, the roar of battle. He stopped the train, and hurried his troops across the fields to the point just where he was most needed. They were at first supposed to be the Enemy, their arrival at that point of the field being entirely unexpected. The Enemy fell back, and a panic seized them. Cheer after cheer from our men went up, and we knew the battle had been won."

Another Rebel correspondent who, as an officer of the Kentucky battalion of General Johnston's Division of the Rebel Army, participated in the battle, wrote to the Louisville Courier from Manassas, July 22, an account of it, in which, after mentioning that the Rebel Army had been forced back for two miles, he continues; "The fortunes of the day were evidently against us. Some of our best officers had been slain, and the flower of our Army lay strewn upon the field, ghastly in death or gaping with wounds. At noon, the cannonading is described as terrific. It was an incessant roar for more than two hours, the havoc and devastation at this time being fear ful. McDowell * * * had nearly outflanked us, and they were just in the act of possessing themselves of the Railway to Richmond. Then all would have been lost. But most opportunely—I may say Providentially—at this juncture, Gen. Johnston, [Kirby Smith it should be] with the remnant of Johnston's Division—our Army, as we fondly call it, for we have been friends and brothers in camp and field for three months—reappeared, and made one other desperate struggle to obtain the vantage-ground. Elzey's Brigade of Marylanders and Virginians led the charge; and right manfully did they execute the work,"]

"The prayer of the wicked availeth not," 'tis said; yet never was the prayer of the righteous more quickly answered than is that of the Rebel General-in-chief! Johnston himself, alluding to this exigent moment, afterward remarks, in his report: "The expected reenforcements appeared soon after." Instead of Patterson's Union Army, it is Kirby Smith, coming up, with Elzey's Brigade, from Winchester!

Satisfied of the safe arrival of Kirby Smith, and ordering him up, with Elzey's Brigade, Johnston directs Kershaw's 2nd and Cash's 8th South Carolina Regiments, which have just come up, with Kemper's Battery, from Bonham's Brigade, to strengthen the Rebel left, against the attempt which we are still making to reach around it, about the Sudley road, to take it in reverse. Fisher's 6th North Carolina Regiment arriving about the same time, is also hurried along to help Beauregard.

But during the victorious lull, heretofore alluded to, something is happening on our side, that is of very serious moment. Let us see what it is:

The batteries of Griffin and Ricketts, at the Dogan House, having nothing to fire at, as we have seen, are resting, pleased with the consciousness of their brilliant and victorious service against the Rebel batteries and Infantry columns, when they are ordered by McDowell —who, with his staff, is upon elevated ground to the rear of our right,—to advance 1,000 yards further to the front, "upon a hill near the Henry House."

Ricketts considers this a perilous job—but proceeds to execute the order as to his own battery. A small ravine is in his front. With Ricketts gallantly leading, the battery dashes across the ravine at full gallop, breaking one wheel as it goes, which is at once replaced. A fence lies across the way. The cannoniers demolish it. The battery ascends the hill near the Henry House, which is full of the Enemy's sharpshooters.

[For this, and what immediately follows, see the testimony of Ricketts and others, before the Committee on the Conduct of the War.]

Soon as Ricketts gets his guns in battery, his men and horses begin to fall, under the fire of these sharpshooters. He turns his guns upon the Henry House,—and "literally riddles it." Amid the moans of the wounded, the death scream of a woman is heard! The Enemy had permitted her to remain in her doomed house!

But the execution is not all on one side, by any means. Ricketts is in a very hot place—the hottest, he afterward declares, that he has ever seen in his life—and he has seen fighting before this.

The Enemy is behind the woods, at the front and right of Ricketts's Battery. This, with the added advantage of the natural slope of the ground, enables him to deliver upon the brave Union artillerists a concentrated fire, which is terribly destructive, and disables so many of Rickett's horses that he cannot move, if he would. Rickett's own guns, however, are so admirably served, that a smooth-bore battery of the Enemy, which has been stubbornly opposing him, is driven back, despite its heavy supports.

And Griffin's Battery now comes rapidly up into position on the left of, and in line with, Ricketts. For Griffin also has been ordered from the Dogan House hill, to this new, and dangerously exposed, position.

But when Major Barry, General McDowell's Chief of Artillery, brings him the order, Griffin hesitates—for he has no Infantry support.

"The Fire Zouaves—[The 11th New York]—will support you," says Barry," They are just ready to follow you at the double-quick!"

"Then why not let them go and get in position on the hill," says Griffin; "then, let Ricketts's and my batteries come into battery behind; and then, let them (the Zouaves) fall back?"

Griffin advises, also, as a better position for his own battery, a hill 500 yards in the rear of the Henry House hill. But advice is thrown away. His artillery-chief is inflexible.

"I tell you," says Griffin again, "the Fire Zouaves won't support us."

"They will," replies Barry. "At any rate it is General McDowell's order to go there!"

That settles the business. "I will go," responds Griffin; "but mark my words, they will not support us!"

Griffin's Battery, indeed, starts first, but, owing to the mistake of one of his officers, it has to be countermarched, so that Ricketts's is thrown to the front, and, as we have seen, first reaches the crest of the Henry House hill.

Griffin, as he comes up with his guns, goes into battery on the left of Ricketts, and at once opens briskly on the Enemy. One of Griffin's guns has a ball lodged in the bore, which cannot be got in or out. His other five guns, with the six guns of Ricketts, make eleven pieces, which are now side by side-all of them driving away at the Enemy's (Stonewall Jackson's) strong batteries, not more than 300 yards away.

They have been at it half an hour perhaps, when Griffin moves two of his pieces to the right of Ricketts, and commences firing with them. He has hardly been there five minutes, when a Rebel regiment coming out of the woods at Griffin's right front, gets over a rail fence, its Colonel steps out between his regiment (now standing up to the knees in rank grass) and the battery, and commences a speech to his men!

Griffin orders one of his officers to load with canister, and let drive at them. The guns are loaded, and ready to fire, when up gallops Barry, exclaiming: "Captain, don't fire there; those are your battery-supports!"

At this supreme moment, Reynolds's gorgeous looking Marines are sitting down in close column, on the ground, to the left of the Union batteries. The showy 11th New York "Fire Zouaves" are a little to the rear of the right of the guns. The gallant 14th New York Chasseurs, in their dust-covered red uniforms, who had followed Griffin's Battery, at some distance, have, only a little while since, pushed finely up, from the ravine at the rear of our batteries, into the woods, to the right of Griffin and Ricketts, at a double-quick. To the left of the batteries, close to the battalion of Marines, Heintzelman bestrides his horse, near some of his own Division.

To Major Barry's startling declaration, Captain Griffin excitedly shouts: "They are Confederates! Sure as the world, they are Confederates!"

But Barry thinks he knows better, and hastily responds: "I know they are your battery-support."

Griffin spurs toward his pieces, countermands his previous order, and firing is resumed in the old direction.

Andrew Porter, has just ridden up to Heintzelman's side, and now catches sight of the Rebel regiment. "What troops are those?" he asks of General Hientzelman, pointing in their direction.

While Heintzelman is replying, and just as Averell drops his reins and levels his field-glass at them, "down come their pieces-rifles and muskets,—and probably," as Averell afterward said, "there never was such a destructive fire for a few minutes. It seemed as though every man and horse of that battery just laid right down, and died right off!"

It is a dreadful mistake that has been made. And there seems to have been no excuse for it either. The deliberateness of the Rebel colonel has given Barry abundant time to have discovered his error. For Griffin subsequently declared, under oath, that, "After the officer who had been talking to the regiment had got through, he faced them to the left, marched them about fifty yards to the woods, then faced them to the right again, marched them about forty yards toward us, then opened fire upon us—and that was the last of us!"

It is a terrible blunder. For, up to this moment, the battle is undeniably ours. And, while the Rebel colonel has been haranguing his brave men, there has been plenty of time to have "passed the word" along the line of our batteries, and poured canister into the Rebel regiment from the whole line of eleven guns, at point-blank range, which must inevitably have cut it all to pieces. The fate of the day hung balanced right there and then—with all the chances in favor of McDowell. But those chances are now reversed. Such are the fickle changes in the fortunes of battle!

Instead of our batteries cutting to pieces the Rebel Infantry regiment, the Rebel Infantry regiment has mowed down the gallant artillerists of our batteries. Hardly a man of them escapes. Death and destruction reap a wondrous and instant harvest. Wounded, dying, or dead, lie the brave cannoniers at their guns, officers and men alike hors du combat, while wounded horses gallop wildly back, with bounding caissons, down the gentle declivity, carrying disorder, and further danger, in their mad flight.

The supporting Fire Zouaves and Marines, on the right and left of our line of guns, stand, with staring eyes and dumb open-mouths, at the sudden turn of affairs. They are absolutely paralyzed with astonishment. They do not run at first. They stand, quaking and panic-stricken. They are urged to advance upon the Rebel regiment—"to give them a volley, and then try the bayonet." In vain! They fire perhaps 100 scattering shots; and receive in return, as they break and run down the hill to the rear, volley after volley, of deadly lead, from the Rebel muskets.

But, as this Rebel regiment (Cummings's 33rd Virginia) advances to seize the crippled and defenceless guns, it is checked, and driven back, by the 1st Michigan Regiment of Willcox's Brigade, which has pushed forward in the woods at our extreme right.

Meanwhile, having been ordered by McDowell to support Ricketts's Battery, Howard has formed his four tired regiments into two lines— Berry's 4th Maine, and Whitney's 2nd Vermont, on the right and left of the first; and Dunnell's 5th, and his own 3rd Maine, under Staples, in the second line. Howard himself leads his first line up the elevated plateau of the Henry House. Reaching the crest, the line delivers its fire, volley after volley, despite the concentrated hail of the Enemy's Artillery and muskets. As the second line advances, a Rebel cannon-ball, and an unfortunate charge of our own Cavalry, scatters most of the 5th Maine. The 2nd Vermont, which has advanced 200 yards beyond the crest, rapidly firing, while the Enemy retires, is now, in turn, forced back by the Enemy's hot fire, and is replaced by the 3rd Maine, while the remnant of the 5th moves up to the extreme right of Howard's now single line. But the Rebel fire grows hotter and hotter, and owing to this, and a misunderstood order, Howard's line begins to dissolve, and then retires in confusion,—Howard and others vainly striving to rally his own utterly exhausted men.

Sherman's Brigade, too, has come over from our left, and now advances upon the deadly plateau, where lie the disabled Union batteries—the prizes, in full sight of both Armies, for which each seems now to be so desperately striving.

Quinby's 13th New York Rifles, in column of companies, leads the brigade, followed by Lieutenant-Colonel Peck's 2d Wisconsin, Cameron's 79th New York (Highlanders), and Corcoran's 69th New York (Irish), "in line of battle." Down the slope, across the ravine, and up, on the other side, steadily presses Quinby, till he reaches the crest. He opens fire. An advancing Rebel regiment retires, as he pushes up to where the Union batteries and cannoniers lie wounded and dying—the other three regiments following in line-of-battle until near the crest, when the fire of the Enemy's rifles and musketry, added to his heavy cannonading, grows so severe that the brigade is forced back to shelter in a roadway leading up the plateau.

Peck's 2nd Wisconsin, now emerges from this sheltered roadway, and steadily mounts the elevation, in the face of the Enemy's severe fire-returning it, with spirit, as it advances. But the Rebel fire becomes too galling. The gray-clad Wisconsin boys return to the sheltered road again, while the cry goes up from Sherman's ranks: "Our own men are firing at them!" Rallying at the road, the 2nd Wisconsin again returns, with desperate courage, to the crest of the hill, delivers its fire, and then, unable to withstand the dreadful carnage, falls back once more, in disorder.

At this, the 79th (Highland) Regiment springs forward, to mount the brow of the fatal hill, swept as it is, with this storm of shot and shell and musket-balls. Up, through the lowering smoke, lit with the Enemy's incessant discharges in the woods beyond, the brave Highlanders jauntily march, and, with Cameron and their colors at their head, charge impetuously across the bloody hill-crest, and still farther, to the front. But it is not in human nature to continue that advance in the teeth of the withering fire from Jackson's batteries, strengthened, as they are, by Pelham's and Kemper's. The gallant fellows fall back, rally again, advance once more, retire again, and at last,—the heroic Cameron being mortally wounded,—fall back, in confusion, under the cover of the hill.

And now, while Quinby's Regiment, on another ridge, more to the left, is also again engaging the Enemy, the 69th New York, led by the fearless

Corcoran, dashes forward, up the Henry House hill, over the forbidding brow, and beyond. As the brave Irishmen reach the abandoned batteries, the hoarse roar of cannon, the sharp rattle of musketry-volleys, the scream of shot and shell, and the whistling of bullets, is at once deafening and appalling, while the air seems filled with the iron and leaden sleet which sweeps across the scorched and blasted plateau of the Henry House. Nobly the Irish Regiment holds its ground for a time; but, at last, it too falls back, before the hurtling tempest.

The fortunes of the day are plainly turning against us. Time is also against us—as it has been all along—while it is with the Enemy. It is past 3 o'clock. Since we last looked at Beauregard's third new defensive line, there have been material accessions to it. The remains of the brigades of Bee, Evans, and Bartow, have been reformed on the right of Jackson's Brigade—Bee on his immediate right, Evans to the right of Bee, and Bartow to the right of Evans, with a battery which has been engaging Schenck's Brigade on the other side of Bull Run near the Stone Bridge; while Cocke's Brigade watches Bull Run to the rear of Bartow. On the left of Jackson's. Brigade, is now to be seen a part of Bonham's Brigade (Kershaw's 2nd South Carolina, and Cash's 8th South Carolina) with Kemper's Battery on its left. Kirby Smith has reached the front, from Manassas, and—in advancing from his position on the left of Bonham's demi-Brigade, just West of the Sudley road, with Elzey's Brigade, in a counter-attack upon our right-is wounded, and carried to the rear, leaving his command to Elzey. Stuart's Cavalry are in the woods, still farther to the Enemy's left, supporting Beckham's Battery. Early's Brigade is also coming up, from Union Mills Ford, not far to the rear of the Enemy's left, with the design of coming into line between Elzey's Brigade and Beckham's Battery, and out-flanking and attacking our right. But let us bring our eyes back to the bloody contest, still going on, for the possession of the batteries of Griffin and Ricketts.

Arnold's Battery has raced up on our right, and is delivering shot, shell, spherical case, and canister, with effect, although exposed to a severe and accurate fire from the Enemy. Wilcox, with what is left of the 1st Michigan, after once retaking the batteries on the plateau, from the 7th Georgia, has got around the Enemy's left flank and is actually engaged with the Enemy's rear, while that Enemy's front is engaged with Franklin and Sherman! But Hobart Ward's 38th New York, which Wilcox has ordered up to support the 1st Michigan, on our extreme right, in this flanking movement, has been misdirected, and is now attacking the Enemy's centre, instead of his left; and Preston's 28th Virginia—which, with Withers's 18th Virginia, has come up to the Rebel left, from Cocke's Brigade, on the Enemy's right—finding the 1st Michigan broken, in the woods, attacks it, and wounds and captures Wilcox. Withers's Regiment has, with a yell—the old "Rebel yell," now rising everywhere from Rebel throats, and so often heard afterward,—

charged the 14th New York Chasseurs, in the woods; and the Chasseurs, though retiring, have fired upon it with such precision as to throw some of their assailants into disorder.

[Says General Keyes, who had kept on down the Run, "on the extreme left of our advance—having separated from Sherman on his right:—I thought the day was won about 2 o'clock; but about half past 3 o'clock a sudden change in the firing took place, which, to my ear, was very ominous. I knew that the moment the shout went up from the other side, there appeared to be an instantaneous change in the whole sound of the battle. * * * That, as far as I can learn, was the shout that went up from the Enemy's line when they found out for certain that it was Johnston [Kirby Smith] and not Patterson, that had come."]

Meanwhile McDowell is making one more effort to retrieve the misfortunes of the day. Lawrence's 5th, and Clark's 11th Massachusetts, with Gorman's 1st Minnesota,—all belonging to Franklin's Brigade—together with Corcoran's 69th New York, of Sherman's Brigade, have been brought into line-of-battle, by the united efforts of Franklin, Averell, and other officers, at our centre, and with the remnants of two or three other regiments, are moving against the Enemy's centre, to support the attack of the Chasseurs—rallied and led forward again by Heintzelman upon the Rebel left, and that of the 38th New York upon the Rebel left centre,—in another effort to recapture the abandoned batteries.

Charge after charge, is made by our gallant regiments, and counter-charge after counter-charge, is made by the fresh troops of the Enemy. For almost half an hour, has the contest over the batteries rolled backward and forward. Three several times have the batteries been taken, and re-taken,—much of the determined and desperate struggle going on, over the prostrate and bleeding bodies of the brave Union artillerists,—but without avail. Regiment after regiment, has been thrown back, by the deadly fusillade of the Enemy's musketry from the skirt of woods at his front and left, and the canister, case, and bursting shells, of his rapidly-served Artillery.

It is now near upon 4 o'clock. Our last effort to recapture the batteries has failed. The Union line of advance has been seriously checked. Some of our own guns in those batteries are turned on us. The Enemy's Infantry make a rush over the blood-soaked brow of the fatal plateau, pouring into our men a deadly fire, as they advance,—while over to our right and rear, at the same moment, are seen the fresh regiments of Early's Brigade coming out of the woods—deploying rapidly in several lines—with Stuart's handful of Rebel Cavalry, while Beckham's guns, in the same quarter, open an oblique enfilading reverse fire upon us, in a lively manner.

At once the minds of the fagged-out Union troops become filled with the dispiriting idea that the exhausting fight which they have made all day long, has been simply with Beauregard's Army of the Potomac, and that these fresh Rebel troops, on the Union right and rear, are the vanguard of Johnston's Army of the Shenandoah! After all the hard marching and fighting they have done during the last thirteen hours,—with empty stomachs, and parched lips, under a scorching sun that still, as it descends in the West, glowers down upon them, through the murky air, like a great, red, glaring eye,—the very thought is terrible!

Without fear, yet equally without hope, the Union troops crumble to groups, and then to individuals. The attempt of McDowell to turn the left of the Enemy's Bull Run line, has failed.

McDowell and his officers heroically but vainly strive, at great personal risk to themselves, to stem the tide of confusion, and disorder. Sykes's battalion of regulars, which has been at our left, now steadily moves obliquely across the field of battle toward our right, to a hill in the midground, which it occupies, and, with the aid of Arnold's Battery and Palmer's Cavalry, holds, while the exhausted and disorganized troops of the Union Army doggedly and slowly retire toward Sudley Ford, their rear covered by an irregular square of Infantry, which, mainly by the exertions of Colonel Corcoran, has been formed to resist a threatened charge of Stuart's Cavalry.

[At the rate of "not more than two, or two and a half, miles an hour," and not "helter-skelter," as some narrators state.]

It is not fear, that has got the better of our Union troops. It is physical exhaustion for one thing; it is thirst for another. Men must drink,—even if they have foolishly thrown away their canteens,—and many have retired to get water. It is the moral effect also—the terrible disappointment—of seeing what they suppose are Johnston's fresh troops from the Shenandoah Valley, without Patterson "on their heels," suddenly appear on their flank and rear. It is not fear; though some of them are panic-stricken, and, as they catch sight of Stuart's mounted men,—no black horse or uniform among them,—raise the cry of "The Black Horse Cavalry!—The Black Horse Cavalry!"

The Union attack has been repulsed, it is true; but the Union soldiers, though disorganized, discouraged, and disappointed, are not dismayed. Their officers not yet having learned how to fight, and themselves lacking the cohesion of discipline, the men have lost their regimental organizations, and owing to the causes mentioned, slowly retire across Sudley Ford of Bull Run, in a condition of disintegration, their retreat being bravely covered by the 27th and 69th New York, (which have rallied and formed there), Sykes's Infantry battalion, Arnold's Battery, and Palmer's Cavalry.

[In his report to Major Barnard, Capt. D. P. Woodbury, of the corps of Engineers, says: "It is not for me to give a history of the battle. The Enemy was driven on our left, from cover to cover, a mile and a half. Our position for renewing the action the next morning was excellent; whence, then, our failure? It will not be out of place, I hope, for me to give my own opinion of the cause of this failure. An old soldier feels safe in the ranks, unsafe out of the ranks, and the greater the danger the more pertinaciously he clings to his place. The volunteer of three months never attains this instinct of discipline. Under danger, and even under mere excitement, he flies away from his ranks, and looks for safety in dispersion. At four o'clock in the afternoon of the 21st, there were more than twelve thousand volunteers on the battle-field of Bull Run, who had entirely lost their regimental organizations. They could no longer be handled as troops, for the officers and men were not together. Men and officers mingled together promiscuously; and it is worthy of remark that this disorganization did not result from defeat or fear, for up to four o'clock we had been uniformly successful. The instinct of discipline, which keeps every man in his place, had not been acquired. We cannot suppose that the troops of the Enemy had attained a higher degree of discipline than our own, but they acted on the defensive, and were not equally exposed to disorganization."]

While the divisions of Hunter and Heintzelman, which came down in the morning across Sudley Ford, are now, with one brigade (Sherman's) of Tyler's Division, retiring again, in this disordered condition, by that ford; two other brigades of Tyler's Division, viz., that of Schenck—which, at 4 o'clock, was just in the act of advancing upon, and across, the Stone Bridge, to join in the Union attack, and of Keyes, which was, at the same time, just succeeding in its effort to turn the right flank of the Enemy's third new line,—are withdrawing from the field, across Bull Run stream, by the Warrenton Pike, and other roads leading them directly toward Centreville. The brigades of both Keyes and Schenck are retiring in good order; that of Keyes, at "an ordinary pace," following close after McDowell, who, with his staff, has ridden across the battlefield and Bull Run; while part of that of Schenck, united with the 2nd Maine (of Keyes' Brigade) and Ayres's Battery, "promptly and effectively" repulses a charge of the Enemy's Cavalry, and covers the rear of Tyler's Division. Both of these brigades reach Centreville, hungry and weary, but otherwise, for the most part, in good shape.

But during this grand all-day attack, by two of McDowell's divisions, directly aided by part of a third, upon the left of the Enemy's original Bull Run line of defense—which attack, while it has failed in its purpose, has also utterly upset and defeated the Enemy's purpose to carry out Beauregard's plan of attacking Centreville that same morning—what has the Left Wing of McDowell's Army been doing? Let us go back to Sunday morning, and ascertain:

All the Army of McDowell, save his Left Wing—which, comprising the two brigades (Blenker's and Davies's) of Miles's Division, and Richardson's Brigade of Tyler's Division that fought the preliminary battle of Blackburn's Ford, is now under the command of Miles,—moved away from Centreville, down the Warrenton Pike, as we have seen, very early in the morning.

Blenker remains with his brigade as a reserve, on the heights a little East of Centreville, to throw up intrenchments; which, however, he does not do, for lack of trenching implements. Richardson and Davies are to make a feint, at Blackburn's Ford, so as to draw the Enemy's troops there, while the heavy blow of McDowell's Right Wing and Centre falls upon the left flank and rear of the Enemy's Bull Run line.

Richardson's Brigade is already down the ridge, in his old position at Blackburn's Ford, when Davies with his brigade reaches it, from Centreville, and, by virtue of seniority, takes command of the two brigades. Leaving Richardson's Brigade and Greene's Battery exactly on the battle-ground of the 18th July, Davies posts two regiments (the 18th and 32nd New York) of his own brigade, with Hunt's Battery, on the brow of a hill, in an open wheat field, some eighty yards to the South-Eastward of Richardson, distant some 1,500 yards from Longstreet's batteries on the Western side of Bull Run,—and commences a rapid fire, upon the Enemy's position at Blackburn's Ford, from both of the Union batteries.

At 10 o'clock, there is a lull in this Union fire. The Artillery ammunition is running short. The demonstration, however, seems, thus far, to be successful—judging by the movement of Rebel troops toward Blackburn's Ford. The lull continues until 11 o'clock. At that time Miles arrives at his front, in a towering rage.

On his way down the ridge, that morning, early, Davies had made a discovery. While passing a roadway, his guide had casually remarked: "There is a road that leads around to the Enemy's camp, direct." "Ah!" — said Davies—"and can they get through that road?" "Oh, yes," replied the guide. Davies had at once halted, and, after posting his 16th and 31st New York Regiments, with two guns of Hunt's Battery, near this road, at its junction with the ridge road running up to Centreville and Black burn's Ford, had proceeded, with the rest of his regiments and guns, to the position where Miles finds him.

But Miles has discovered what Davies has done, in this matter of the flanking roadway; and—without knowing, or apparently caring to know, the reason underlying the posting of the two regiments and two guns in its vicinity,—flies into "a terrible passion" because of it; in "no very measured language," gives Davies "a severe dressing down;" and orders him to bring both regiments and guns down to the front. Davies complies, and says nothing. Miles also orders him to continue the firing from his batteries, without regard to the quantity of ammunition. This order, also, Davies obeys—and the firing proceeds, for two solid hours, until another order comes, about 1 o'clock P.M., to stop firing.

The fact is, that Miles is not at all himself—but is suffering under such a strain of mental excitement, he afterward claims, that he is not responsible.

Miles, however, returns to Centreville about noon; and no sooner is he gone, than Davies at once sends back pioneers to obstruct that road which would bring the Enemy around his left flank and rear, to Centreville. These, work so industriously, that they cut down a quarter of a mile of trees, and block the road up completely. Davies also posts a few pickets there, in case of accidents. It is well he does so. It is not long before the Enemy makes an attempt to get around to his rear, by that road; but, finding it both obstructed and picketed, retires again. Davies does not see the Rebels making that attempt, but catches sight of them on their return, and gives them a severe shelling for their pains.

Davies keeps up his firing, more or less—according to the condition of the Enemy and of his own ammunition—until 4 o'clock, when the firing occasioned by the Union flanking movement, six miles to his right, ceases. Then there reaches him a note from Richardson, so badly penciled that he can only make out the one word "beaten,"—but cannot, for the life of him, make out, whether the beaten one is our Right Wing, or the Enemy!

Of what followed, he tells the story himself,—under oath, before the Committee on the Conduct of the War—so graphically, that the temptation to give it, in his own words, is irresistible. "I saw unmistakable evidence," said he, "that we were going to be attacked on our Left Wing. I got all ready for the attack, but did not change my front.

"About 5 o'clock, I think, the Rebels made their appearance back upon this very road up which they had gone before; but instead of keeping up the road, they turned past a farm-house, went through the farm-yard, and came down and formed right in front of me, in a hollow, out of my sight. Well, I let them all come down there, keeping a watch upon their movements. I told the Artillery not to fire any shot at them until they saw the rear column go down, so as to get them all down in the little hollow or basin, there. There was a little basin there, probably a quarter of a mile every way. I should think that, maybe, 3,000 men filed down, before I changed front.

"We lay there, with two regiments back, and the Artillery in front, facing Bull Run. As soon as about 3,000 of the Enemy got down in this basin, I changed the front of the Artillery around to the left, in face of the Enemy, and put a company of Infantry between each of the pieces of Artillery, and then deployed the balance of the regiments right and left, and made my line-of-battle.

"I gave directions to the Infantry not to fire a shot, under any circumstances, until they got the word of command from me. I furthermore said I would shoot the first man that fired a shot before I gave the command to do so.

"I gave them orders all to lie down on their faces. They, (the Rebels) were just over the brow of the hill, so that, if they came up in front of us, they could not hit a man.

"As soon as I saw the rear column, I told * * * Lieutenant Benjamin to fire. * * * He fired the first shot when the rear column presented itself. It just went over their heads, and hit a horse and rider in their rear. As soon as the first shot was fired, I gave the order for the whole six pieces of Artillery to open with grape and canister. The effect was terrible. They were all there, right before us, about 450 yards off, and had not suspected that we were going to fire at all, though they did not know what the reason was. Hunt's Battery (belonging to Richardson—who had by mistake got Greene's) performed so well, that, in thirty minutes, we dispersed every one of them!

"I do not know how many were killed, but we so crippled their entire force that they never came after us an inch. A man, who saw the effect of the firing, in the valley, said it was just like firing into a wheat field; the column gave way at once, before the grape and canister; they were just within available distance. I knew very well that if they but got into that basin, the first fire would cut them all to pieces; and it did. We continued to fire for thirty minutes, when there was nothing more to fire at, and no more shots were returned."

At a later hour—while remaining victorious at their well defended position, with the Enemy at their front, dispersed and silenced,—these two brigades of the Left Wing, receive orders to fall back on Centreville, and encamp. With the brigade of Richardson, and Greene's Battery in advance, Davies's own brigade and Hunt's Battery following, they fall back on the heights of Centreville "without the least confusion and in perfect order"—reaching them at 7 P.M.

Meantime Miles has been relieved from command, and McDowell has ordered Blenker's Brigade to take position a mile or more in advance of Centreville, toward Bull Run, on both sides of the Warrenton Pike, to protect the retreat, now being made, in "a few collected bodies," but mainly in great disorder—owing partly to the baggage-wagons choking the road, along which both venturesome civilians and fagged-out troops are retreating upon Centreville. This confused retreat passes through Blenker's lines until 9 o'clock P.M.—and then, all is secure.

At midnight, McDowell has decided to make no stand at Centreville, but to retire upon the defensive works at Washington. The order to retreat, is given, and, with the rear well guarded by Richardson's and Blenker's Brigades, is carried out, the van of the retreat, with no Enemy pursuing, degenerating finally into a "mob," which carries more or less panic into Washington itself, as well as terrible disappointment and chagrin to all the Loyal States of the Union.

Knowing what we now do, concerning the Battle of Bull Run, it is somewhat surprising, at this day, to read the dispatches sent by McDowell to General Scott's headquarters at Washington, immediately after it. They are in these words:

"CENTREVILLE, July 21, 1861—5:45 P.M.

"We passed Bull Run, engaged the Enemy, who, it seems, had just been re-enforced by General Johnston. We drove them for several hours, and finally routed them."

["No one who did not share in the sad experience will be able to realize the consternation which the news of this discomfiture—grossly exaggerated—diffused over the loyal portion of our Country. Only the tidings which had reached Washington up to four o'clock—all presaging certain and decisive victory—were permitted to go North by telegraph that day and evening; so that, on Monday morning, when the crowd of fugitives from our grand Army was pouring into Washington, a heedless, harmless, worthless mob, the Loyal States were exulting over accounts of a decisive triumph. But a few hours brought different advices; and these were as much worse than the truth as the former had been better: our Army had been utterly destroyed-cut to pieces, with a loss of twenty-five to thirty thousand men, besides all its artillery and munitions, and Washington lay at the mercy of the Enemy, who were soon to advance to the capture and sack of our great commercial cities. Never before had so black a day as that black Monday lowered upon the loyal hearts of the North; and the leaden, weeping skies reflected and heightened, while they seemed to sympathize with, the general gloom. It would have been easy, with ordinary effort and care, to have gathered and remanded to their camps or forts around Alexandria or Arlington, all the wretched stragglers to whom fear had lent wings, and who, throwing away their arms and equipments, and abandoning all semblance of Military order or discipline, had rushed to the Capital to hide therein their shame, behind a cloud of exaggerations and falsehoods. The still effective batteries, the solid battalions, that were then wending their way slowly back to their old encampments along the South bank of the Potomac, depressed but unshaken, dauntless and utterly unassailed, were unseen and unheard from; while the panic-stricken racers filled and distended the general ear with their tales of impregnable intrenchments and masked batteries, of regiments slaughtered, brigades utterly cut to pieces, etc., making out their miserable selves to be about all that was left of the Army. That these men were allowed thus to straggle into Washington, instead of being peremptorily stopped at the bridges and sent back to the encampments of their several regiments, is only to be accounted for on the hypothesis that the reason of our Military magnates had been temporarily dethroned, so as to divest them of all moral responsibility," Greeley's Am. Conflict, pp. 552-53., vol. I.]

"They rallied and repulsed us, but only to give us again the victory, which seemed complete. But our men, exhausted with fatigue and thirst, and confused by firing into each other, were attacked by the Enemy's reserves, and driven from the position we had gained, overlooking Manassas. After this, the men could not be rallied, but slowly left the field. In the meantime the Enemy outflanked Richardson at Blackburn's Ford, and we have now to hold Centreville till our men can get behind it. Miles's Division is holding the town. It is reported that Colonel Cameron is killed, Hunter and Heintzelman wounded, neither dangerously.

"IRWIN MCDOWELL,

"Brigadier-General, Commanding.

"Lieutenant-Colonel TOWNSEND."

"FAIRFAX COURT HOUSE, July 21, 1861.

"The men having thrown away their haversacks in the battle, and left them behind, they are without food; have eaten nothing since breakfast. We are without artillery ammunition. The larger part of the men are a confused mob, entirely demoralized. It was the opinion of all the commanders that no stand could be made this side of the Potomac. We will, however, make the attempt at Fairfax Court House. From a prisoner we learn that 20,000 from Johnston joined last night, and they march on us to-night.

"IRWIN MCDOWELL.

"Colonel TOWNSEND"

"FAIRFAX COURT HOUSE, [July] 22, 1861.

"Many of the volunteers did not wait for authority to proceed to the Potomac, but left on their own decision. They are now pouring through this place in a state of utter disorganization. They could not be prepared for action by to-morrow morning even were they willing. I learn from prisoners that we are to be pressed here to-night and tomorrow morning, as the Enemy's force is very large, and they are elated. I think we heard cannon on our rear-guard. I think now, as all of my commanders thought at Centreville, there is no alternative but to fall back to the Potomac, and I shall proceed to do so with as much regularity as possible.

"IRWIN MCDOWELL.

"Colonel TOWNSEND."

"ARLINGTON, July 22, 1861.

"I avail myself of the re-establishing of telegraph to report my arrival. When I left the forks of the Little River turnpike and Columbia turnpike, where I had been for a couple of hours turning stragglers and parties of regiments upon this place and Alexandria, I received intelligence that the rear-guard, under Colonel Richardson, had left Fairfax Court House, and was getting along well. Had not been attacked. I am now trying to get matters a little organized over here.

"IRWIN MCDOWELL.

"Brigadier-General.

"E. D. TOWNSEND."

McDowell had unquestionably been repulsed, in his main attack, with his Right Wing, and much of his Army was badly demoralized; but, on the other hand, it may be well to repeat that the Enemy's plan of attack that same morning had been frustrated, and most of his forces so badly shattered and demoralized that he dared not follow up the advantage which, more by our own blunders than by his prowess, he had gained.

If the Union forces—or at least the Right Wing of them—were whipped, the Enemy also was whipped. Jackson himself confesses that while he had, at the last moment, broken our centre, our forces had turned both of his flanks. The Enemy was, in fact, so badly used up, that he not only dared not pursue us to Washington—as he would have down had he been able—but he was absolutely afraid McDowell would resume the attack, on the right of the original Bull Run line, that very night! For, in a letter to General Beauregard; dated Richmond, Virginia, August 4, 1861, Jefferson Davis,—who was on the ground at Bull Run, July 21st,—alluding to the Battle of Bull Run, and Beauregard's excuses for not pursuing the Union troops, says:

"I think you are unjust to yourself in putting your failure to pursue the Enemy to Washington, to the account of short supplies of subsistence and transportation. Under the circumstances of our Army, and in the absence of the knowledge since acquired—if, indeed, the statements be true—it would have been extremely hazardous to have done more than was performed. You will not fail to remember that, so far from knowing that the Enemy was routed, a large part of our forces was moved by you, in the night of the 21st, to repel a supposed attack upon our right, and the next day's operations did not fully reveal what has since been reported of the Enemy's panic."

And Jefferson Davis's statement is corroborated by the Report of Colonel Withers, of the 18th Virginia, who, after starting with other regiments, in an attempt to cut off the Union retreat, was recalled to the Stone Bridge,—and who says: "Before reaching the point we designed to occupy (near the Stone Bridge) we were met by another order to march immediately to Manassas Junction, as an attack was apprehended that night. Although it was now after sunset, and my men had had no food all day, when the command to march to Manassas was given, they cheerfully took the route to that place."

Colonel Davies, who, as we have seen, commanded McDowell's stubborn Left Wing, was after all, not far wrong, when, in his testimony before the Committee on the Conduct of the War, he declared, touching the story of the Bull Run Battle: "It ought to have read that we were victorious with the 13,000 troops of the Left Wing, and defeated in the 18,000 of the Right Wing. That is all that Bull Run amounts to."

In point of fact, the Battle of Bull Run—the first pitched battle of the War—was a drawn battle.

War was now fully inaugurated—Civil War—a stupendous War between two great Sections of one common Country; those of our People, on the one side, fighting for the dissolution of the Union—and incidentally for Free Trade, and for Slavery; those on the other side, fighting for the preservation of the Union—and incidentally for Protection to our Free Industries, and for the Freedom of the Slave.

As soon as the Republican Party controlled both Houses of Congress it provided Protection to our Free Industries, and to the Free Labor engaged in them, by the Morill Tariff Act of 1860—the foundation Act of all subsequent enactments on the subject. In subsequent pages of this work we shall see how the Freedom of the Slave was also accomplished by the same great Party.

www.ingramcontent.com/pod-product-compliance
Lightning Source LLC
Chambersburg PA
CBHW070750290526
45795CB00002B/549